TRUE FACTS

comics'
righteous
anger

LARRY YOUNG

TRUE FACTS
BY LARRY YOUNG

PUBLISHED BY
AIT/PLANET LAR
2034 47TH AVENUE
SAN FRANCISCO, CA 94116

FIRST EDITION APRIL 2002

10 9 8 7 6 5 4 3 2 1

WWW.AIT-PLANETLAR.COM

COVER DESIGN BY BRIAN WOOD
COVER PHOTOGRAPH BY JULIAN CASH

ISBN: 0-9709360-9-5

PRINTED AND BOUND IN CANADA BY QUEBECOR PRINTING, INC.

TRUE FACTS

comics'
righteous
anger

LARRY YOUNG

AiT/Planet Lar
San Francisco

for Mimi and Bri

who talked me into it

Introduction

I've been accused of ripping off a lot of people in my day, but the only one I can ever cop to aping consciously is a guy named Lester Bangs.

Bangs was a rock writer out of Detroit. He was a speed-freak lover of R O C K, and his passion for it practically bled off the page. He wrote seminal articles on The Greatest Bands in the World; he went toe-to-toe with Lou Reed on a routine basis; he toured with the Clash and reported with a startled, awestruck sincerity at meeting Rock Stars he actually liked. The trick was Bangs didn't write about what he heard-- he wrote about what he felt; he weaved his own life into his work and the result was that we had a rock critic not in an Ivory Tower of commentary, but rather a sorta fucked-up uncle that rambled on and on with a zeal equally hysterical and exhausting. He was street-level. He was like you or me. He was a fan.

Bangs died too soon. Bad drugs and bad health, of course, but his legacy lives on in his writing; some of those pieces will last forever:

"(Patti Smith's) sound is as new-old as her look. You hear the Shangri-Las and other early Sixties girl groups, as well as Jim Morrison, Lotte Lenya, Anisette of Savage Rose, Velvet Underground, beatniks and Arabs. Meanwhile, the minimalism of the band forces her sound out front along with the poetry, and that sound stands. This is not a 'spoken-word' album, it's a rock'n'roll album, and even if you couldn't understand a word of English you couldn't miss the emotional force of Patti's music. And you'll love it when she makes mistakes (in this era of slick, pre-digested 'rock' as muzak), when her voice goes ragged (but right), like the perfect act of leaping for something precious. Who needs the other kind of perfection?"

Bangs wrote with a clarity and passion that made me, as a sixteen and seventeen year old kid, go out and seek what he was talking about. If these bands, this music, could make THIS guy feel THAT GOOD... what would it do to me?

See, this is the thing about Bangs' work: Good writing is good writing. Good writing is compelling and compulsive, regardless of its subject matter, whether it's Bangs writing about the MC5 or Ed Regis writing about Mambo Chicken Breeding or a young Ernest Hemingway writing about the day he went to Barber College for a free haircut:

"Upstairs is where the free work is done by the beginners.

"A hush fell over the shop. The young barbers looked at one another significantly. One made an expressive gesture with his forefinger across his throat.

"'He's going upstairs,' said a barber in a hushed voice.

"'He's going upstairs,' the other echoed him and they looked at one another.

"I went upstairs."

How can you NOT turn that page, I ask?

I've always thought that voice -- a clear, resonant, and interesting voice -- was the most important tool any writer can have. It's probably the hardest thing to teach or to learn, too. On my weaker or more weary days, I don't think Voice can be taught at all, but rather is the very gift of writing itself, the soul of the

8

entire art. A good writer will make me read anything, regardless of my interest in what they've written about.

This was my one and only real editorial tenet when I worked for the webzine SAVANT as an editor (terribly superficial and subjective, is it not? Well, why not? I wasn't dumb enough to think of myself as a journalist; I was a fan.). There was a depressing lack of interesting voices talking about comics, talking about the medium and its potential, talking about this strange, fucked-up field that I've found myself drawn to artistically and professionally for the last few years. Comics are just as vital and exciting to me as music… so where was our Lester Bangs?

SAVANT began as a lament (I'm assuming it was a lament, even though I personally took it as a dare) from writer Warren Ellis. Wondering aloud why there was no NME or MELODY MAKER-esque 'zine on comics, he set certain wheels spinning across the web. One Sunday night me and some other folks dove in headfirst to try and make such a thing exist.

Whereas I can't speak for the writers I edited or the other editors working along side of me, I very rarely cared about what was being written so much as how it was being written.

What bothered me enough to get involved with SAVANT is that most comics writing left me cold. How could such a medium as comics, a medium that's stimulated, excited, challenged and fascinate me as much as it has NOT have unique voices talking about them?

So then. We started SAVANT. I wanted my bits to read like one part *Cashier Du Cinema* and one part *Creem*. If I had an agenda beyond the self-serving, get-my-name-out-there angle of it (which I've never denied and, god help us all, seems to have worked a little bit), it was that I wanted to be responsible for helping something into the world that was written in such a way that someone could pick a copy up at random, feel the ache and drive in-between the paragraphs that we all felt for comics, and get their asses right fucking now to a comic shop to see what all the fuss was about.

The same way Bangs led me to Patti Smith, the Clash, or the Velvet Underground once upon a time.

The problem was that... well, who the fuck were we? Nobodies. Digital phantasms, asserting a cocky and brash Something out of the Nothing of cyberspace. We were speaking by the virtue of being heard, really; the observation of SAVANT was what made SAVANT work. Through all the posturing and poseur hyperbole, I knew that we weren't really anyone other than fans with rampaging egos, thesauri, and web access. And, while not necessarily a deal-breaker, this little truism certainly didn't escape my attention or egomaniacal concern.

Enter Larry Young.

Shortly after we launched, Larry dropped me a line and proposed a column. TRUE FACTS, as he wanted to call it, would document everything anyone would need to know about self-publishing. And, since DO IT YOURSELF was a SAVANT mantra (re-purposed from punk, of course), it made perfect sense. We were all about Something From Nothing, right? We were about self-determination. We were about showing off that anyone with a thought in their head could get it Out There if they wanted.

Larry had responded to our manic bombast, and we

responded to both the weight that came with his name (let's be honest, eh?) and the Message he wanted to get out there. The only thing we had ever done was SAVANT, right? But Lar... Lar was doing it himself. He had begun building his very own comics empire, and now he wanted us to help him tell the world how to follow suit.

This isn't to say that everyone who wrote or writes for SAVANT wants to do comics, but you have to admit there's a certain lack of understanding from those of us who were there that did. The idea of a DIY guide was just the sort of practical thing I felt we needed.

But.

There are few things that say STAY AWAY like a How-To guide. Who among us have ever put a technical manual down with an exhausted, satisfied sigh and declared, "WOW! I wanna read that AGAIN!"

Exactly.

I knew Larry as a web presence, I knew Larry as the guy Kurt Busiek called "the Johnny Appleseed of Comics." I knew him as a bullshittin', shit-shootin', sarcastic and *funny* fucking bastard that really, REALLY loved what he did. I'd read his comics, so I knew he could write those, but... a How-To guide? We're... I thought we were all trying to smash our guitars before getting the third chord out, you know? Who the hell cares how to play an F-sharp, man? What if TRUE FACTS was stuffy? What if it was clinical? What if it was... *boring?*

I was nervous, waiting for the first column to arrive. Would a How-To column by Lar actually sound like the Lar I knew? And if it didn't... who the hell was *I* to tell him it didn't? But lo, and behold... there was

Larry's voice, and I was a fool for doubting it'd be absent.

TRUE FACTS broke the rule. Above and beyond its educational value (which is why you're reading this collection, and not any of the namby-pamby artsy-writer bullshit I'm droning on and on about, I know), it was readable. Enjoyable. Witty, funny, inspiring, even.

It was a *narrative,* for Christ's sake!

Most of all, TRUE FACTS was more than a bunch of wannabes talking about how great comics were; it was a column that made you feel how great comics were, written by a guy who knew because he taught himself. Not because he just felt it, no no -- Larry Young *knows.*

Larry sounded like we sounded, and reading TRUE FACTS like getting tricked into learning.

So now then: YES, you're holding in your hands a book that will teach you everything that can be taught about self-publishing comics, from the philosophical to the practical. YES, you will be as armed as anyone could ever be after reading this collection to get into comics on your own. YES, each and every question that CAN be answered IS answered. When you're finished, there will be no more that anyone can teach you; the rest is experiential, waiting out there for you to find it, live it, and learn it.

But it's a *great* goddamn read. Thanks, Lar.

Matt Fraction
Kansas City
January 2002

one

Please allow me to introduce myself; I'm a man of wealth and taste.

Actually, "wealth" is a bit of a stretch. And come to think of it, I thought *Armageddon* was a kick-ass movie, so that claim to "taste" may be off a bit, as well.

Still.

Maybe you've seen me around. Maybe you've been in for a pint on Friday with me and the boys at Comix Experience in San Francisco, where I'm the wise and terrible Minister of Propaganda, and talked about comics. Maybe you've read the *Astronauts in Trouble* comics I've written for Charlie Adlard to draw. Maybe you've seen some of my stuff online.

The thing is, in comics... I'm around. I do EVERY-THING but draw my comics, so I've got the creative side covered. I do pre-press and print management for my own publishing house; you may have heard AiT/Planet Lar is publishing the former Oni mini *Nobody* and the former Image mini *Channel Zero*. So there's publishing and distribution taken care of: check. I do marketing and promotions for one of the top ten comic stores in the country, and ride the counter ten hours a week, to get a flavor of what retailers and readers alike are into. So there's retailing covered.

Damn, when you see it all written down like that, I'm a friggin' comic book Renaissance Man.

But I've had a lot of email lately asking me for THE SECRET. The HOW'D YOU DO THAT? And, of course, the ol' I WANT TO DO A COMIC TOO.

And it began to occur to me that I was answering

about four or five different emails six thousand times. Everyone wants to know the same thing. And since I'm a heckuva guy when I'm not pissed off, I figure I'll address some of these things for you. Spread my hard-won experience around. Show you the mistakes I made so you don't have to make 'em.

It's my opinion, sure; but it's opinion based on around seventeen years of working in comics retail, print publishing, and advertising and marketing. I pay attention. So should you.

So let's assume you want to do a comic book. Get ready for some harsh truths. If you want to go get a Coke, or a beer, or a tablespoon of NyQuil, go ahead.

Steel yourself, because I'm gonna hit you with The Big One:

Want to do a comic?

Go ahead.

Nobody's stopping you.

One of the most attractive things about the comic book form, to me, is that any monkey with an opposable thumb, a decent magic marker, and some typing paper can make his own damn self a funny book.

Everything else is just a matter of SCALE. So, let's say you're still on board. Doing a comic sounds good to you. "But I need an IDEA," I can hear some of you saying. You people, I can't help you. If you don't have an idea for which you are ready to sweat blood onto a page, there's nothing I can do. The rest of you? Over here: split yourselves into artists and writers. That's where we'll start.

OK, writers: *write.* That's it. Write your idea down. Sculpt it, spew it, finesse it; it doesn't matter. Put it down. Beginning, middle, end. Now read it. Does it read professionally to you? No? Then go rewrite until it does.

Lather. Rinse. Repeat.

Ready to tackle the script? A page a day gives you a twenty-two page comic in just over three weeks. Think about that for a second.

Don't watch *Friends* this week. Give *U-571* a miss until it hits cable. Tell yer pals there is no pizza in your future. Don't buy that *Encino Man* DVD. In three weeks AT THE MOST you'll have a comic book script for an artist to draw.

All right; artists. Got your metaphorical pen poised? Draw a car. A football. A tree. A girl. Now draw the car from three-quarters left and ten feet above. Draw the football in the hand of a quarterback, close up. Now draw eight panels, one right after another, of the camera pulling back with the football as the quarterback cocks his arm to throw downfield. Now do the same thing from the POV of the FOOTBALL. Draw the tree like George Perez, because god DAMN if you don't look at a George Perez tree in *The Avengers* and say to yourself, "Well, now, that's a TREE." Draw the girl who sat next to you in third grade, looking up and talking to herself as an adult. Does all that look professional to you? Perspective, angles, dramatic camera shots?

All right; good. Next week, I'll get you guys fluent with the language of pre-press, which is what you'll need once you artists and writers get together and actually *produce* your 22 pages.

But, for now. Write. Draw. Get together and feed each others' creativity. You all are on your way.

And that, my friends, is a TRUE FACT.

●●●●●●●●●●

Not much to add to this one, really, which was just supposed to be an introductory column. Bit of a gauntlet throw, and a call to action. Just a little from-me-to-you to try to inspire those reading who were on the fence about producing their own comics. Sometimes all the cool cats need when they're on the fence is a firm shove in one direction or another, yes?

Two years later, I no longer do promotions for Comix Experience. I run the publishing house full-time, and as of right this second we've produced eight comic books, sixteen trade paperbacks, two original graphic novels, a hardcover book of photography and prose, four patches, two jackets, five T-shirts, two posters, a watch and a baseball cap.

We have projects in the pipeline to produce one a month from now until August of 2004.

If you're reading this book, you're probably doing your own comics. A first thought may be, "Does AiT/Planet Lar accept submissions?"

The short answer is, no, not really.

We have a lot of stuff in the hopper, and a comic by an unknown is a tough sell. This is what I heard when I was shopping around the astronauts, and it's still true today. But if you have a completed, pencilled, inked, and lettered seventy-two page graphic novel, go ahead and send it to me to see what I think. Although, if I were you, I'd publish it my own self.

two

All right. Last week, you read the first installment of this column, and you got all fired up, didn't you? You sat down and you crafted a compelling tale. Let's say you've lived a just life, and, for the sake of argument, you've got 22 pages of comic book entertainment you want the world to see.

What now?

If you don't want to invite your friends over to your house to read the art boards one at a time, you're gonna have to get the thing printed, so folks around the world can have copies of your genius. Then that begs the question, "How do we get copies of my comic into the hands of discriminating comic fans everywhere?" The answer to that is "distribution." How will your receptive audience know to stop watching *Two Guys and a Girl* and get to a comic store to actually purchase your tale of heartbreak and triumph? Marketing.

See? You thought doing a comic was EASY.

Your job's not done when you've written and drawn it, oh no.

This week, we'll tackle the next step: Pre-press and printing. Now, "pre-press" is exactly what it sounds like. It's all the hoops and hurdles you have to jump through to get your comic book pages assembled in the proper order for your printer to turn it into a comic book. But don't get excited, cha-cha; you need to know who's PRINTING your book first because printers have idiosyncratic ways of doing the same thing, and you need to be speaking their language. One printer might say "four-color" while another might say "key plus three." And believe it or not, they're talking about the same thing. So instead of explaining the entire history of printing in the 900 words the

Savants have given me, I'm gonna get you talking to one printer.

First, you need to quote your job out to a couple places, because you want to get the best price, or the best quality, or the most convenient-for-you printer. Now, when we were quoting out *Astronauts in Trouble: Live from the Moon #1*, we sent our specs to ten printers, all found by studious online research, and narrowed the field down to three:

Brenner Printing Co.
1234 Triplett
San Antonio, TX 78216
Fax: 210 349 1501

Morgan Printing
402 Hill Ave.
Grafton, ND 58237
Fax: 701 352 1502

Quebecor Printing
8000 Blaise-Pascal Ave.
Montreal Quebec H1E 2S7
Fax: 514 881-0276

We went with Quebecor for several reasons. They're the largest printer in North America; they print a lot of Marvel, DCs, Image, and Oni books, so they know what a comic book looks like; the cost-per-unit was a little higher than the others, but they ship directly to Diamond's warehouse in Plattsburgh, so that's a savings on shipping; and my print rep, Olga, the woman who has to deal with me, is the coolest, most professional print rep I've ever dealt with in my seventeen years of dealing with print reps. So there you go. Choose what works best for you.

To quote a job, you have to give the printer an exact

idea of what you want the printed comic to look like. You need to specify the number of pages your book will have; the paper stock of the interiors as well as that of the cover; what sort of binding the book will have; how it will be packaged and shipped; how you will deliver the artworks and materials (whether they will shoot the film to make the printing plates directly from your artwork, or output the art from computer files straight to film); and how many (the print run) you want.

As an example, *AiT: Live from the Moon #1* was a pretty standard comic book. It had 24 interior black and white pages, plus a four-color cover. The spec: 24 B&W (1/1) plus cover (4/1). That means in addition to your 24 pages of comic INSIDE, you've got a cover, an inside front cover, and inside back cover, and a back cover to provide to the printer. For the paper stock, we used 50# offset for the interiors and 70# coated for the cover. Again, pretty standard. Don't use newsprint (28-35#) whatever you do; the ink soaks through and it looks pretty cheesy. Don't worry if you don't get paper grades right now; these are all things that a good print rep will help you with.

The binding is saddle-stitched; that's your basic "staples." It's called saddle-stitching because they aren't staples at all; the folded, collated comic is fed along a V-shaped bar (the "saddle") and an immense needle threaded with wire pops down and hits your comic twice.

Now, "delivery" sort of steps into the spotlight of next week's "distribution" column. Until then, let's just say that we specified delivery to the Plattsburgh Diamond warehouse of the initial purchase order, with the balance of the print run shipped to the AiT/Planet Lar World Headquarters in beautiful San Francisco.

For artworks and material, we supplied the original art, clearly labeled with page number for the strippers to shoot for film. If you think when I wrote "strippers" I was referring to folks who take off their clothes for money, I refer you to International Papers' Pocket Pal: A Graphic Arts Production Handbook, because you need to know more about printing than I can cover with the 200 or so words I have left. Matt Hollingsworth's cover color files were supplied to the printer on Mac CDs in final cover files on which I worked up titles, graphics, and logos. That one's gonna be specified by the needs of your printer, as well.

You also need to indicate who gets to see the blue lines, which are a mock-up of the comic printed with photo-sensitive paper to check the layout and quality of the films shot for making your printing plates. This intermediary step allows you to catch and correct errors before the final product is printed.

Then, finally, you need to specify your print run. Since this is your first job quote, ask to see the prices on runs of 1000, 3000, and 5000. That'll give you an idea of how much paper and printing costs go, and is a realistic low-and-high-end assessment of how many comics you'll sell right out of the gate in the direct market.

So, get your information together, draft a cover letter asking the printer to quote a job with your specs you've provided, TYPE IT UP, and fax it to the attention of the "New Accounts Representative." Wait a couple of days or so, and you should have some answers. You're one step closer to seeing all of that hard work in *a book*. That idea you had is that much closer to assuming actual form.

And that, my friends, is a TRUE FACT.

three

We're halfway there. You've finally got printed copies of your comic in your hands. You've made some effort, cleared some hurdles, but there's still some hard work before you. So, now's a good time to take a metaphorical look around and take stock of the situation whilst girding your figurative loins for what's to come, because the rest of the trip comes fast and simultaneous.

In fact, you can look at it like you're at the base camp of Mt. Everest. You've done a whole lot of training and acclimating to get where you are, but the *real* climb is ahead of you.

And to make that climb, or to get your comic out there for the world to see, is to join an almost self-contained society of misfit idealists. A sense of community is absolutely engendered within a group so unnoticed by the rest of the world. But getting to the top of that mountain, or giving your comic book physical form, is not considered very important to your clan of fellow adventurers. No, it is the how of your trip which resonates; the obstacles overcome, the lessons learned, the logistics tackled in a bold and unflinching style.

And in mountaineering, as in comics, no one is more admired than the free soloists; those who climber Jon Krakauer calls "the visionaries who ascend alone." But we're at the base camp now, and we're gonna need some serious support to finish the rest of the way. And some of that support will come from your distributors. But go ahead and smile your secret grin as you get yourself ready for the climb, because we're halfway there.

Let's assume, for the sake of argument, that Diamond Comics Distributors has accepted your comic for distribution. This, you can assure, by sending copies of it for review to:

Steve Leaf
Diamond Comics Distribution
1966 Greenspring Drive
Timonium. MD
21093

But Steve and his review board will read over your work and deem it professional-looking and worthy of inclusion in *Previews* (the retailer/consumer catalog in which the comic-book-reading audience first sees books offered for purchase). Because, if they don't, you're pretty much out of luck. Diamond serves most of the retailers in the U.S.

When they accept your comic for solicitation, you, as publisher, will get a quite informative packet explaining payment terms, delivery, solicitation guidelines, and all sorts of interesting, arcane, and esoteric minutiae about the distribution process. As soon as you get this pack, memorize it. There's more useful info in that package than almost any single other thing I've read. And you will need to know everything in it, because you're "tested" on your knowledge every month that you solicit. If you drop the ball on something, it's your fault, not Diamond's. And, in the unlikely event it is Diamond's fault, it doesn't matter, because it's your responsibility. No one will care about your comic more than you do, so stay on top of it. And if an error does occur, don't *blame* anyone. *Fix it.* Anything else looks unprofessional.

So, three months before you've gone to print, Diamond has provided you with a publisher liaison (mine's Chris Schaff, and a more professional rep I could not have asked for) and solicited your comic. Retailers have a month to place their orders, Diamond counts up the data, and issues you a purchase order a month after that. A purchase order tells you how many copies to print. I always over-print the P.O. by a few percentage points to allow for reorders.

So, you call your print rep with the distribution numbers. Diamond breaks down their purchase orders by warehouse. They presently have eight warehouses spread out amongst the U.S., and the P.O. you get will have the amount of copies going to each warehouse. Give this info to your print rep, and have any overage sent to you, so you'll have some copies to fulfill reorders and sell at conventions and keep for your Memorial Library you'll no doubt be building with all the money you make from your comic.

At the same time you send out your initial request for inclusion to Diamond, you'll also want to send the same package to at least two other places:

Wayne Markley
FM International
913 Stewart Street
Madison, WI 53713

and
Tim Stroup
Cold Cut Distribution
475-D Stockton Ave.
San Jose, CA
95126

FM was formed out of the ashes of the late and lamented Capital City Distribution, if I'm not mistaken, and represents a "protest vote" amongst retailers uncomfortable with Diamond's ubiquitousness. Cold Cut is a little like an after-market auto parts shop, where they do good business supplying retailers with copies of still-sellable comics that have gone past Diamond's 30-60 day sales window. All three do right by me, and I recommend you get on their good sides, because if they don't carry your book, you're gonna be hard-pressed to make money long enough to expand into other, non-direct market vendors.

Just as last week my printing column stepped a little into distribution, so this column will step into next week's one on marketing. Since you're most likely reading this column on www.savantmag.com, it's probably safe to say you're at least passingly savvy when it comes to the Internet.

I cannot recommend highly enough using the Internet as a tool to create buzz for your product, provide a 24 hours a day access to information and other content about your comic, and as a tool to sell your comic directly to readers who can't find it. The sad fact about the direct market in the year 2000 is that most retailers won't initially order your comic.

It's an industry truism that 10% of the comic book stores are moving 90% of the comics, and next week, I'll show you some ways to target those stores specifically. But, for now, you've got your comic in the distribution pipeline, and that means you're that much further up the mountain.

And that, my friends, is a TRUE FACT.

●●●●●●●●●●

All the names and contact info in this one are still current, so don't be afraid to send copies of your comic to these folks. One thing, though; Chris Schaff moved over to toys, and our Diamond Brand Manager is now Fil Sablik: the hardest-working man in comics.

four

Last week I promised you a paean to the Internet, and its role in good comic book marketing. Specifically, I wrote: "I cannot recommend highly enough using the Internet as a tool to create buzz for your product, provide a 24 hours a day access to information and other content about your comic, and as a tool to sell your comic directly to readers who can't find it." That is, of course, a TRUE FACT.

But when girding my figurative loins to begin this column, the thought occurred that I may have been reading ahead. We've covered the creative side, the pre-press and printing, the distribution of comics. The next step should be marketing your comic, right?

Well, it is. Make no mistake. But since this is the bit that most creative types either sidestep or flat-out ignore, we're gonna slow the tempo down here a little and start at the very beginning.

Sit back and let your Wild Uncle Lar get you hip to branding.

"Branding" is just what it sounds like. The big ol' red-hot poker cowboys used to sear the mark of the ranch into the side of their cattle. Now, you've got a metaphorical side of beef, or a comic book, that you want to put out into the world. And since the world is one big long scream for attention in this media-saturated Year of Our Lord Two Thousand, the only hope you have of having your high-quality comic stand out on the shelf from all the other high-quality books that have survived the If-You-Build-It-They-Will-Come of the speculator-driven frenzy that was the Comic Book Industry ten years ago... the ONLY hope you have...

...is a strong brand.

Now, you're lucky. Building a strong brand is a lot

easier with the advent of the worldwide audience you have access to on the Internet. Before the Internet garnered the global access it enjoys today, it took companies DECADES and billions of dollars to build a strong brand. Now, a focused zealot with fat pipes and a clear connection can build a strong brand in a matter of weeks with his only investment being time spent in front of the computer.

But how do you go about building your brand? Well, you have to decide what you're going to try to put across with your comic. You're going to have to decide what you're about; what we refer to here around the AiT/Planet Lar World Headquarters as "pick a pitch and swing." Just as in baseball a successful hitter doesn't wildly take stabs at whatever is thrown across the plate, you're going to have to realize your comic can't be all things to all people. Not everyone likes anchovies on their pizza, after all. So you smooth this out by staying true to your brand. What's the brand? You'll have to answer that for your own project. But I can tell you what a brand is not.

A brand isn't an icon, or a catchy slogan, or a mission statement, or a manifesto, or a Photoshopped logo. A brand is a promise your company keeps in every decision you make, every ad you place, every Internet posting, every interaction at any level with your public. Your brand is your identity and it is your reputation.

Look at Visa. The blue and gold logo is your assurance that they're everywhere you want to be. Disney's Mickey-Mouse-ears silhouette invites you to experience the magic. Coke adds life. Do you Yahoo? All of these invoke strong associations with strong brands. Lucky for you, just starting out, you can do the same thing these mega-corporations did just by using the Internet.

But first, put some thought into what you're going to project. Make sure that the identity of your comic is clear in your head, because you won't be able to communicate to others if you have a fuzzy view of what you're trying to put across. *Astronauts in Trouble,* for example, is a paper movie you can roll up and put in your back pocket. I knew I was clear on that message when ubiquitous Internet presence Adrian Brown wrote me that *AiT* was "the comic that made him forget Bruce Willis made action films."

Second, know that what you offer your reader is value for their time. Make sure that you understand that time spent reading your comic is time the reader could be doing something else, and celebrate your readers' good taste for choosing to spend their time with you and your work. Warren Ellis is a master of this. With his every cranky albeit good-natured inter-action with his audience, Ellis reinforces, in an almost-deceptively charismatic way, that time spent reading his work is a value returned above even that of the high quality entertainment offered within. Reading a work of Ellis is not just enjoyable escapism; it's reinforcement that you're a Member of His Club. You could do worse than taking a page out of *that* book, believe me.

Third, and probably most important, you have to stay consistent with adherence to your brand. The symbols you choose, the imagery, the metaphors, even down to the colors on the website you no doubt will have to promote your comic... over time these all will help to reinforce your brand identity...

...but you have to be consistent. Your brand is your face to the outside world. A *solid* brand is the cor-nerstone to successful marketing.

And that, my friends, is a TRUE FACT.

five

Selling comic books isn't like selling cans of oil.

Maybe you'll recall that in addition to writing and publishing, I do marketing and promotions for one of the top ten comic stores in the US, Comix Experience. Maybe you'll further recall that I mentioned (way back in TRUE FACTS #1) that on Fridays, between 11 am and 2 pm, you can come into the store and have a beer with me and talk about the funny books.

Usually, it isn't nearly as degenerate as it sounds; three or four or five regulars come in for their new comics and bring me beer and we sit and we drink and we solve the comic book industry's problems. If you want an idea of a typical My Friday Pint With Larry ™, click here:

http://www.lazybastard.com/fridrep2a.htm

The point is, getting lit with the customers on Friday afternoon doesn't much happen at the oil can store, y'know?

So comics are a special case. And the selling of said comics even moreso.

Take, for example, the writing of press releases. In the real world, the writing of press releases and their dissemination is a study in media manipulation. Buy this brand of diapers. Jeff Goldblum tells you to switch to AT&T. Dead John Wayne is gumped into beer ads. And you know what?

There's absolutely no reason why you can't use the same sort of tactics to get the word out about YOUR comic. There's no reason to do all the work involved to write, draw, print, and distribute your comic if you're not going to keep following through on the backswing and help the retailers SELL it to a waiting audience.

The easiest way to help the retailers sell your book is to let 'em know it's available, and the easiest way to do that is to write an informative and easy-to-digest press release.

Now, there are all sorts of guides and helpful dos and don'ts for writing press releases available with even the most cursory of searches on the Internet, so I'll just give you the overview of how *I* do it:

1. I write FOR IMMEDIATE RELEASE across the top. This lets your folks know that the information contained within is ready to go whenever they are ready to use it. It's a call to action.

2. I put in my CONTACT DETAILS. Name, company, email address, phone number. That one's pretty self-explanatory.

3. The HEADLINE should be pretty short and pithy. I use the ol' No More Than Eight Words rule, but, that said, I break it all the time. The press release I wrote announcing *Channel Zero*, though, was pretty catchy: "Tune in to Channel Zero"

4. Next, I put a little explanatory line of copy to whet the journalists' appetites. The CZ one was "AiT/Planet Lar to publish acclaimed socio-political miniseries collection."

5. Your FIRST PARAGRAPH should follow the "pyramid" structure. The first bit has the main point. Up front, concise; maybe even sums up the whole point of the press release in one sentence: "Publisher Larry Young announced today that his publishing house, AiT/Planet Lar, has acquired the trade paperback

rights for the former Image Comics miniseries Channel Zero."

6. Then I like to air it out a little; just picture it as starting at the top of the pyramid and traveling down to the ground. It broadens and widens out: "Socially-conscious and politically-aware, this quick trip into the present-future shows us the between-click world where the Freedom of Speech is sooo Twentieth Century. Written and drawn by acclaimed comics creator Brian *(Generation X)* Wood, the award-winning Channel Zero shows television to be the tool of the government, where propaganda-laden sitcoms and infomercials flood the airwaves. Reduced to gumption-less couch potatoes, society has lost the will to resist. Armed with a camcorder and a laptop, Jennie 2.5 leads the fight to regain control of the airwaves, and bring the power back to the people." That sort of thing.

7. Put two or three short paragraphs explaining the story for the body of the press release. It helps to have quotes from comic book industry bigshots showing you the love. Even a simple quote from you saying why you're doing the project gives a human dimension to the dry facts. I get a little silly in this part of the release because I realize I'm providing content for comics news websites and print magazines, and anything you can do to stand out from the other press releases will get your stuff out there under the eyeballs of the retailers and fans.

8. It doesn't hurt to type "-30-" or "###" at the bottom of your release to let the journalists know you're finished.

OK, so you're done writing your press release. You've checked it over for typos and grammar. You're sitting back, scanning it again, well-impressed with what you've crafted. In fact, you're looking at the Greatest Press Release in Human History. Now what?

You've gotta have an email contact list. About a year before I began publishing, I started canvassing the Internet. People were putting out all sorts of press releases, and weren't too hip on how their email programs worked. My pals Rob Snell, of Gun Dog Comics and Brian Hibbs, of Comix Experience, were only too happy to help me get what I was looking for, and started forwarding me emails that they'd received from other publishers that had HUNDREDS of email addresses attached to which they'd been cc'd. I remember Todd McFarlane's company sent Hibbs one that had nearly every comic book industry bigshot's email address.... and they *weren't* blind-copied!

In less than two months, I had collected in an Excel document over 4000 minty-fresh email addresses of retailers, fans, and pros. Not to mention the media contacts.

You've got to assemble your own project-specific email list, but THESE guys should help you get the word out when it's time to start hyping your comic:

WIZARD:JMcLauch@aol.com

COMIC SHOP NEWS: cliffbig@earthlink.net

COMICS BUYER'S GUIDE: cbgnews@krause.com

DIAMOND COMICS DISTRIBUTORS:
bvince@diamondcomics.com

FM INTERNATIONAL: mfbway@aol.com

COLD CUT DISTRIBUTION: thompson@coldcut.com

COMIC BOOK RESOURCES:
news@comicbookresources.com

COMIC CONTINUUM: RobAlls@aol.com

NEWSARAMA:
mbrady669@aol.com, newsarama@aol.com

SEQUENTIAL TART: pr@sequentialtart.com

Heck, go ahead and put ME on your list, too. I love reading comic book industry press releases. I'm at: larry@ait-planetlar.com

All of these cats love comics as much as you do, and are extremely helpful in getting the word out about comics they love. A well-written press release just makes their jobs easier. Write a good press release, and you'll get good coverage.

And that, my friends, is a TRUE FACT.

●●●●●●●●●●

When I read the comic book news websites every morning, after my run down to the beach, I am constantly amazed at the things folks write press releases ABOUT. It's a rare month when you DON'T have a "press release" about a late book that's off-schedule because a creator stubbed his toe in the bathroom or had the flu or had to take his kid to school. And that just slays me. Everyone has things in their personal lives to deal with; it's what you accomplish AROUND life's problems that separates the men from the boys.

If I could relate any bit of good advice to fledgling comics creators, it'd be this: "Play hard, be nice, have fun... and DO THE JOB." The world doesn't need more bellyachers; it needs more good comics.

six

Now is the time on Sprockets when we dance.

Because of the fluid nature of the comic book industry; heck, because of the fluid nature of life itself, whenever I think I know what next week's column is going to be about, something happens at Comix Experience, or I get some odd piece of news at the AiT/Planet Lar World Headquarters, or somebody lets slip some juicy piece of gossip and I'm off to the races with my take on whatever shiny object strikes my fancy.

This week is no different.

I was checking in on Randy Lander's superlative comic book discussion forum:

www.delphi.com/snapjudgments

when erstwhile comics pundit Zack Smith asked me a killer question: "How the hell does one get noticed as a writer in this industry?"

Now, at first, I was tempted to answer archly something like, "just paint yourself green and duct tape proposals to your ass as you prance around naked in front of Mike Carlin at DC's booth in San Diego." And while it's hard to see how that WOULDN'T make you stand out, I'm pretty sure that ol' Mike wouldn't hire you for the next *Legends of the Dark Knight* fill-in.

But after a couple of shots of that low-down Tennessee sippin' whiskey, it began to occur to me that not only would Jack Lord have made a better Captain Kirk than William Shatner... not only is Sela Ward a handsome woman but a talented actress as well... not only can Charlie Adlard draw anything I can think up...

...but it finally filtered in to what I laughingly call "my brain" that Zack's somewhat frustrated question and the answer thereto might very well make a nice fit with the previous TRUE FACT columns on marketing and promotion and branding and press releases that I've done so far. Because, really, what is "making yourself stand out" if not effectively marketing and promoting yourself and your talent?

OK, so let's assume that you have a high-quality proposal and an above-average level of talent and writing skill, because it's extremely difficult to get noticed in the comic book industry as a writer. There are industry veterans who have trouble getting editors to return their calls, much less actually offer them work.

So you're competing for spots that already have talented folks vying for them, and if you're not up to that yet, keep scribbling until you believe you can step up to the plate and face the big leagues.

But there are some things you can do.

One of the things that really sticks in my mind that someone did to get themselves noticed was a double-whammy from my pals Jim Pascoe and Tom Fassbender. Fassbender was formerly the product manager at the dearly-missed Capital City Comics distribution house, and then editor of the Image/Motown line. Pascoe was the assistant to the general manager of the San Diego Comic Book Convention, and the two lads decided to strike out on their own.

Forming Uglytown Productions, which you can find on the web at:

www.uglytown.com

...Fassbender and Pascoe wrote a pulp-style detective story called *By The Balls,* and got Paul Pope to provide interior illustrations. But, knowing that the marketing and promotion of the project might be a little dicey, what with mainstream folks not recognizing their names and, at best, having a vague idea who Pope was... coupled with comic book readers not really knowing what to make of such a hybrid/illustrated prose, since it hearkened back to the days of, dare I say it, pulp fiction (this was a few years before Chris Golden's *Hellboy* book and the advent of such things as *Frightening Curves*)... well, Fassbender and Pascoe realized they'd have their marketing cut out for them.

So what'd they do? To make their project, and, by extension, themselves, stand out from the crowd?

Well, Fassbender and Pascoe descended on the Alternative Press Expo like supernatural evangelists. Everywhere you looked that year, Tom, Jim, and the slightly-frazzled, deer-in-the-headlights Paul Pope were ALL OVER the floor of the con. The first decision they made that increased their visibility was that they opted NOT to get a table and be just another set of guys in the crowd... but decided instead to use a little shoe leather and tread the floor of the show spreading the good word about their project.

The second decision they made took a little advance planning, but paid off in spades.

Tom and Jim weren't rubes, and had spent a little time in the industry getting to know who's who and what's what. Getting their proverbial hands dirty in the metaphorical trenches, Tom and Jim figured out how to tell comic book time without looking at the big clock.

So, being able to anticipate who the editors, publishers, and industry-opinion-leaders were that were probably going to attend the show, Tom and Jim were able to make up a little press kit, a project summation, what Brian Michael Bendis and his Hollywood boys call a "take-away." Something that describes the project in detail; ideally has copies of the proposal or, even better, actual copies of the finished book. Fassbender and Pascoe provided a copy of four or five Paul Pope illustrations, Xeroxes of the first three or four chapters of *By The Balls*...

...and this is the important part...

...sealed them...

...in a 9" x 12" white envelope with the word "confidential" stamped across the front...

...and a small Avery-brand sticker pre-printed with the recipient's name.

Think about that for a second.

Say you're, I dunno, Axel Alonso, DC editor extraordinaire and visionary of the Vertigo line. You're eating a corn dog and swilling a beer and trying to get back to your post at the DC booth at this year's San Diego con, and somebody comes up to you and says, "Hey, Axel, bubala, I have a great idea for a Vertigo-style *Captain Carrot* miniseries."

If that's all you've got, ol' Axel will politely excuse himself and retire to a more private place to eat his corn dog. But if you say, "Excuse me, Mr. Alonso, I can see you're enjoying that fine culinary experience, and I'd really not want to take up your time nor divert you from your sustenance... but I have the World's Best Comic Book Story contained right here in this

little white envelope... and I know your time is valu-
able, and you've got a lot of stuff going on at this convention... but I wonder if you wouldn't give this a read
on the flight home and give me a call when
you get back to New York."

If that package you leave with your targeted editor
has "Confidential" stamped across the top, and his or
her own name pre-printed on it (indicating that you
had to do a little advance aforethought with the proposal)...

I can tell you...

...that editor will at least read your stuff. And if it's
GOOD stuff, that's half the battle.

And that, my friends, is a TRUE FACT.

●●●●●●●●●●

*Reviewer Randy Lander doesn't much post to his
snap judgments board on delphiforums.com anymore, as he and Don MacPherson have started up an
even-more-superior comics review site:*

http://www.thefourthrail.com

*Updated almost daily, these guys are the real deal,
and have their fingers on the pulse of mainstream
comics as well as the more esoteric fare.*

*Former Vertigo editor Axel Alonso is now practicing
his trade across town under the watchful eye of
Marvel Comics.*

*It is unknown whether or not Axel actually does enjoy
corn dogs.*

seven

Who pays the bills?

I was sitting outside the other day, keeping a careful eye on the $60 water sprinkler I had just bought to water (lovingly and with a minimum of fuss and strain) the Kentucky Bluegrass I had just planted in the backyard of the AiT/Planet Lar World Headquarters, and as I was reclining in a fog of, well, fog (we are in San Francisco, after all), I had occasion to read an interview with Brian Singer, the director of the upcoming X-Men motion picture extravaganza.

The interview was in the latest issue of *Cinefantastique*, which is a movie-review mag whose emphasis is on coverage of the films of s-f, horror, and other odds bodskins of that stripe. Cinema of the fantastique, I guess; hence the name.

But the point is that this isn't a comic book industry trade magazine; it's a magazine about film.

And in this interview, in the THIRD PARAGRAPH of the whole article, Singer felt the need (without prompting from the interviewer) to make this statement: "My partners are huge [X-Men] fans, and I do nothing, repeat, nothing, without their full support. I have the perspective of someone who's coming in fresh, just trying to make a good movie. I have objectivity, but I also have the consultation of people who are fanboys. So you can tell all the fanboys who are [writing about me on the Internet] that I'm approaching this like a fanboy."

Now, why the director of *The Usual Suspects* feels the need to make this sort of statement is really quite beyond the scope of my little screed here. I will make note that even if EVERY SINGLE PERSON who buys the UNCANNY X-MEN goes to this film on opening day, that'll account for only around 1.5 million dollars of the film's take.

But if I had to guess as to why Singer was quoted thusly?

I'd say that he knows who pays his bills.

He understands that if the word of mouth on his $75 million art house flick isn't EXTREMELY strong, Hollywood's gonna have a Dolph Lundgren *Punisher* on its hands instead of a Tim Burton *Batman*.

And Singer understands that the word of mouth, at least initially, will be led by the people in the audience who care about the quality of this film.

They *want* to enjoy it. But they will be merciless if Singer and his ilk don't deliver.

And now we apply this to comics.

Who pays the bills?

The publishers? Well, they foot the bill for creative and for advertising, marketing, and production, sure. But where's THAT money come from?

The readers and fans who buy the comics? Well, kinda, sure; but if your book's not in the store, you can have a block-long line of customers with cash in hand but if your book's not there, they can't buy it.

Distributors, then? Nope. It's true that if the distributors aren't doing their jobs, customers can't buy your comic, but if the distributor isn't doing his job, he's only shooting himself in the foot.

No, you know who pays the bills?

Retailers.

If you have a comic book of your own that you want to market and promote effectively, your Wild Uncle Lar is gonna hit you with another one of his patented shockers:

Forget advertising.

Get yourself a half-page ad in *Previews* to accompany your solicitation in the month that it appears there, sure; you want to be taken seriously after sweating your blood onto a page for your book. But other forms of advertising is a waste of money, initially.

There's an old industry saw that 10% of the retailers are buying 90% of the comics, and I'm here to tell you that's exactly right. And with a little bit of elbow grease on your part, it's not a secret who these guys are.

And now, thanks to Mark S. Adams, it's not that hard to find out how to get in touch with them, either.

Mark does a great site; heck, he supplies a comic book PUBLIC SERVICE at

www.the-master-list.com

It's a pretty comprehensive site, and lists as many comic book stores and their contact info as can be determined by one hard-working man.

So, spend a little time on the Internet. Hang out on Delphi, troll through the brackish waters of Usenet for useful info, ask your local retailer who he thinks the opinion leaders in retailing are. And then target those guys with your book, because those are the guys that will stock it.

I'll give you a few, in no particular order: Comix Experience and Comic Relief in San Francisco and Berkeley, CA, respectively; Atlantis FantasyWorld in Santa Cruz, CA, and Flying Colors in Concord, CA. Golden Apple and Meltdown in Los Angeles. Comickaze in San Diego.

Zanadu in Seattle, Washington. Big Planet and Beyond Comics in Maryland. Lone Star and Titan Books in Texas. Quimby's in Chicago. Dr. No's in Atlanta. Big Brain in Minneapolis. Comicopia in Boston. Heroes and Dragons in South Carolina. Jim Hanley's Universe and St. Mark's and Midtown in NYC.

And that's just OFF THE TOP OF MY HEAD. You can find a million places where they'll be happy to at least LOOK at your comic. If it's a high-quality piece of funny book entertainment, you can bet they'll want to hear more from you, and then it's up to you to leverage that interest.

Send 'em promo stuff, original artwork for raffles and incentives; posters, whatever they want. Ask a retailer who likes your book what sort of thing would help generate interest for it in his shop. Does his store hang posters? Does it do well with ancillary items? Make t-shirts with your book's logo, and GIVE 'em to the guy!

This is where most guys starting out with their own comics tend to run out of steam, because they've worked inhumanly just to get the damn book to the point where it's done and printed... BUT YOUR JOB'S NOT OVER! You've got to sell it, to recoup your initial investment and to turn a tidy profit.

But if you ignore the retailer, he'll ignore you. There's too much demand for his time to go chasing after every monkey who's done a comic. The retailer has been burned too many times.

But God bless each and every person who's still got an open store in this, the bleakest time for comics in the last fifty years. Because you can bet the farm that anyone with a store that's successful in this climate is someone who not only loves comics but is someone who knows what they're doing.

And if you can prove that you'll meet 'em half-way by making a quality comic, and putting it out WHEN YOU SAY YOU WILL and be available to try new and innovative things to make your book stand out and sell in their store...

Well.

Retailers are the people in the audience who care about the quality of their entertainment. They *want* to enjoy it.

But they will be merciless if you don't deliver.

But retailers are happy when they make money.

You will be happy when you make money.

You will be happy when RETAILERS make money, because then they realize, hey! This comic isn't selling so badly, so they bump up their orders by a few copies, and then you make MORE money.

But don't forget the retailers. Those are the guys who are in the trenches, behind the counter, fighting the comic book war. Ya gotta take care of your boys.

And that, my friends, is a TRUE FACT.

eight

Be the bunny.

Sounds weird, I know, since you've been used to reading some well-chosen, and, dare I say it, entertainingly erudite bits of wisdom from me about publishing and marketing comic books; but I've got no better advice for you. Last October, the missus and I went to the wedding of *Transmetropolitan* artist Darick Robertson. Using powers of persuasion rivaling only those of Jedi Master Yoda, Darick somehow convinced the otherwise levelheaded and no-nonsense Meredith Miller to spend the rest of her life with him.

Now, the nuptials were what the society pages call a "resplendent affair." Quaintly nestled in the heart of Golden Gate Park in San Francisco, and directly across from the deYoung Museum, is a band shell. You've seen the kind of thing I'm talking about, either on Bugs Bunny or PBS.

It's one of those great big concave half-beach-ball-looking things wherein bands and orchestras and plays are performed outside. The kind of place where you'd be just as likely to hear the Boston Pops perform the Imperial March triplets from the score of *The Empire Strikes Back* as you would some poor high school senior screaming out Lady Macbeth's soliloquy on a Saturday afternoon because he lost a bet with his English teacher.

But, of course, this being San Francisco, nothing is ever utilitarian or functional without a bit of the ornate thrown in, like too much mascara on a girl (or *boy*, I guess, this being, after all, San Francisco) who's pretty to begin with; so the band shell is not only perfectly acoustically engineered but constructed within a set of columns and doodad-ery evocative of the ancient Greeks and their architecture.

So, I'm setting the stage, so to speak, here. Bear with me.

Arrayed in a level space before the band shell and its attendant stage is a set of wooden benches set in rows and in a semi-circle facing the stage. It is here that the wedding's guests sat and witnessed the proceedings.

On the stage itself were chairs for the family members and the wedding party. Darick had on the usual standard-issue morning coat, and Meredith was stunning in her wedding gown. Darick's groomsmen had tux jackets and kilts, and Meredith's bridesmaids had lovely eggplant-colored matching dresses. All pretty much by-the-Martha-Stewart-wedding-book, so far.

As the temperature dipped so far down that the fog started to roll in and my wife's fingers literally started turning blue (this being San Francisco, in October, and at six at night), you may be unsurprised to learn that things turned decidedly ice cold and yet Fellini-esque, and I was put of the mind to understand a key concept in comic book storytelling:

Ya gotta be the bunny.

Parenthetically, those who know me may think they know where I'm going with this one, in that the affable yet tilting Brian Hibbs (proud owner of Comix Experience) is wont to refer to DC Comics as "The Bunny" because of Warner Brother's use of Bugs Bunny on the DC folks' expense account credit cards. But that is not the bunny to which I refer.

No, this night, at Darick and Meredith's wedding...

...not only was the man who married them old and infirm and had to be wheeled in to perform the ceremony, but he was dressed outlandishly and brought in on a throne of such high craftsmanship to be just on the pleasant side of ostentatious...

...not only were the girls who wheeled his throne down the ramp to the center of the stage the sexiest sex-bombs you'd ever see outside of 1970s Dallas Cowboys Cheerleaders calendars, but they were also dressed as Catholic Bishops...

...not only were the guests serenaded by a guy who flew in from ITALY to regale us with dead-perfect Paul McCartney tunes...

..not only did John *(The Bod)* Heebink (a guy who SMELLS liquor and wants to fight the biggest guy in the room) actually drink EIGHT glasses of really good red Italian wine and was filled not with his usual ire, but with the milk of human kindness...

...not only were all of these sights and sounds per-sonally witnessed by me...

...but there was also a guy dressed as the Easter Bunny.

Now, ordinarily, I have no trouble with folks showing up to events dressed as secular icons. You can't have a parade in San Francisco, no matter what time of year, without some folks showing up dressed as Santa Claus, or Uncle Sam, or the pets.com sock puppet dog. No problem with that whatsoever.

But inside of three minutes of his first appearance, the guy with the bunny suit took his head off for a breath of fresh air.

My nearly frozen-wife instantly leaned over to me and whispered, "Oh,that's too bad. Doesn't he know the importance of being the bunny?"

I had to sagely nod at her comment.

What's this gotta do with comics, you may well ask?

Well, first, the guy in the bunny suit was Darick's pal Andre, most well-known around these parts as the physical manifestation of Spider Jerusalem in Warren Ellis and Darick Robertson's *Transmetropolitan*. To see what a good job Darick does capturing his likeness, click here:

http://www.transmetropolitan.com/images/andre.jpg

But second of all, it's a lesson for us all. Yes, Life Is To Be Led Out Loud. Yes, Passion demands passion. Yes, we should all go loony every once in a while. General Electric chairman and CEO Jack Welch doesn't go in for half-measures when charting success for his company. You can't behave in a calm, rational manner. You've got to be out there on the lunatic fringe in order to be successful at whatever it is you do, because everyone else has got rationality taken care of.

But if you're gonna show up at a public function in a bunny suit, you've gotta COMMIT. You've gotta prance around, play with the little kids, torment the guys and flirt with the girls. But. You. Always. Have. To. Be. The. Bunny.

And if you've put out a comic book into the wheezing marketplace today, you're at a wedding in a bunny suit. You're there to entertain.

Don't forget it. Get all self-righteous about "your art"and "your story to tell" and "your clear vision,"sure; but do me a favor.

Keep your head on straight.

Be the bunny, and you can't go wrong.

And that, my friends, is a TRUE FACT.

●●●●●●●●●●

This one got a whole lot of attention; I think it's because after nearly two months of weekly updates, an audience had started to form; plus, with the mention of Darick Robertson's wedding, I think many Transmet *fans had checked out the column. This one also got one of the* strangest *responses to any of my columns, and I think I got a little taste of what real celebrities go through: the day this one first was posted on the Internet, I was riding the counter at Comix Experience. A reader called me at the shop to thank me for telling him, personally, to be the bunny.*

"What?" I said, never having ever spoken to the person before. I barely had an idea who he was. Even after *he had introduced himself, at my request, I only had the slightest recollection of seeing his name on the comic book discussion boards.*

"Your Savant article made me knuckle down and get a project off the ground," he said.

"Congratulations," I answered, because I really didn't have anything more to say than that.

There's a pause. Then it got longer.

And then I almost hung up, because, y'know, I was at a retail shop where people actually wanted to buy things, when he said, "So, um..."

I interrupt him, because this sort of thing drives me

mental. "Look, unless I know you, I'm just not a chattin' on the phone kind of guy. I'm at work, here. If you have something to say, spill it."

"Um... Uh, don't you want to know what the project is?"

"I have to go," I said, and the heck of it is, I really did, because someone was trying to buy Astronauts in Trouble: Space 1959. That cracked me up. I wasn't even pushing it; I had to get off the phone to sell a copy of my own book I thought that was just hysterical.

"Um," he continued, when I didn't say anything more. I don't have a lot of time for indirect people anymore. Not that I ever did, but still. Even less, now.

"I'm the only guy up for writing a particular film-to-comic book adaptation," he said.

""Well, it looks like you won't have much competition, then. Good luck with it."

"Um, yeah," he said.

"Look, I gotta go," said I.

"Er, I just wanted to thank you again."

"OK, you're welcome," I said.

"Um, bye," he said.

I just didn't have the heart to tell him he didn't get the point of being the bunny. That being the bunny is a commitment to entertainment; not just talking about doing something. Two years later, even an announcement of his project has still not surfaced.

nine

I've assembled you all here because there's a war on. I know some of you squeamish cats are a little hesitant to embrace the militancy of the metaphor, but a fact's a fact.

There's a war on.

If you've been following the ebb and flow of the comics industry for as long as I have, you've seen these ups and downs before. Interest drives sales, followed by the inevitable drop. I've seen this happen four major times since 1981. ALWAYS something happens to renew interest in the form. *Maus* wins its Pulitzer, the *Teenage Mutant Ninja Turtles* become ubiquitous, *Superman* dies. And comics are hip and cool again.

Well, I don't know if you noticed, but comics aren't recovering on their own this time. It's the best time, creatively, for comics. Folks are doing frankly innovative things with sequential entertainment. But there's a war on. A war for your audience's attention.

Bigger men than us have tried to tackle this problem. They haven't been getting very far.

There're are a few folks who think they've got a handle on it, and they call themselves the New Vanguard. On the delphi.com forums (or, more correctly, "fora"), there's a guy named Kevin Feeley. He started up a discussion forum to try to make some sense about comics, and try to get a few like-minded people together to make some funnybooks. In the course of some discussions there, I tried to light a fire under Kevin's ass by trying to make him see that he and his pals at the Combustible Muse Assembly are the new vanguard of comics.

"What do you mean by that?" Kevin asked.

I wrote "The Diatribe of the New Vanguard" for him

http://www.comicbookresources.com/columns/index.c
gi?column=cia&article=388

and the name just sort of stuck.

Go read it. It's not a manifesto; it's a call to arms.

So we grunts in the trenches are making our comics. We're shutting u and putting up. Since the old guard seems to be failing us, we've taken matters into our own hands. And I wanted to see what the guys who are fighting the good fight had to say.

I asked them this question: "What's it like being on the front line of innovation in funny books and the last best hope for the form?" Here's what I heard back.

Mal Jones, art editor, NextComics.Com: "It means I have the chance to do things RIGHT. Sure I'm going to fuck up, but being part of the frontline in this comic blitzkreig is letting me learn hard and fast how to get work done RIGHT. It means I have a chance to get things out there and tell stories in a way they need to be told. Now if you will excuse me, Sarge, I have to get back into the trenches. There's comics to make."

Scott J Grunewald, www.popimage.com publisher: "Right now, it just makes me feel like I don't have to go to the big two to succeed in comics. It gives me the impression that I can do it on my own. And it makes me feel like I can get away with some of mad, insane stuff. It just makes me feel like I have a chance."

Bryan O'Malley, artist, *Couscous Express:* "I keep

wanting to jump up and down and giggle like a little girl. Is that unbefitting of a soldier? Other than that—it gives me a whole lot of hope that I can not only make a living from comics, but actually eke out a meaningful existence, too. Push meaning and love into people's hearts."

Antony Johnston, writer, *Rosemary's Backpack*: "When I was 19, I realized that what I wanted to do in life was jump up and down on tables, shouting. I wanted to do something which made a difference, artistically, no matter how small or large. I wanted to do something which would make people think, and maybe even inspire someone to do the same. But mostly I just wanted to jump up and down on tables."

Writer/publisher of Broken Boy and the Combustible Muse Anthology, Scott O. Brown: "The New Vanguard means the future. It means we've collectively seen the problems and decided they will not be a barrier to the stories we need/want to tell. The New Vanguard is strength in numbers, because one man cannot conquer the multiverse, even if his parallels are on his side. And I will do my part to instigate change and never stop telling my stories.":

Drew Gilbert, artist, *Rosemary's Backpack:* "I have a larger platform to get everyone's attention, and hopefully hold it. I have a support group where I feel great supporting everyone, knowing I'll be shown love right back. I have a place where we figure out what's wrong, and do our best to remedy the situation. I no longer have any real desire to work for anyone who will try to make me work in ways I don't care to."

Writer (and Combustible Muse Host) Joe Szilagyi: "It means being able to tell my stories without worrying about the so-called 'standard'. It means worrying about how to do things better rather than good enough. It means we're not running the same race as the rest of the industry. We're designing our OWN race, that WE set the rules to. And most importantly to me, it means we're going to change things to the right way, in the end."

Ladies and gentlemen, it's these guys and others like them that are the future of comics. Join us. Not to put too fine a point on it, your stories will save an industry.

And that, my friends, is a TRUE FACT.

●●●●●●●●●●

Two years later, and nothing much came of the whole New Vanguard call-to-arms. When my pal Guy Vardaman had a gig as the Klingon gunner in Star Trek VI, *all of his friends were jealous. "Being a Klingon is a much cooler thing to* have done *than to actually* do," *Guy said then, and I think that was the problem with the New Vanguard cats. Doing comics seemed like a more fun thing to talk about doing than to actually do, for those guys.*

But:

In the intervening two years, Mal Jones drew a graphic novel, Overtime, *for Scott Brown's Cyberosia Press. Scott Grunewald is still publisher of PopImage. Antony Johnston wrote* Frightening Curves, *also from Cyberosia, although* Rosemary's Backpack, *his work with Drew Gilbert, has yet to appear.*

Bryan O'Malley drew eight pages of Couscous Express, *and was replaced by artist Brett Weldele for the published graphic novel, much like that Eric Stolz/Michael J. Fox thing during the production of* Back to the Future.

ten

L.A. Times reporter Pam Noles asked me these questions about promoting comics at a panel at the big San Diego Comic Book Convention. These are my answers:

Why did you decide to pursue publicity outside of the standard comics arena?

I think anything that can draw real-world attention to comics in general is a good thing. If attention is brought to the comics I publish in particular, well, so much the better.

If you had never chased down wider publicity in the past, what made you decide to do it now?

We've spent A LOT of money investing in our publishing house, and marketing, promotion, and publicity are three obvious tools available to a company to try to profit from the initial investment.

Did you give greater or lesser weight to traditional media outlets or Internet-based news sources?

Initially, I skewed much heavier to Internet-based news sources, because I was more familiar with what drives the news on comic book-based news sites. In the course of putting that plan into effect, I learned that traditional media are just as content-starved as Internet-based news sites. It's a natural progression. Plus, it's easier to pitch news stories to newspapers, magazines, and television if you can point to a place where you've been an object of attention. The interview I set up for Brian Wood in October's *Wired* magazine, to spotlight AiT/Planet Lar's edition of *Channel Zero* was a direct result of my being interviewed on CNN editor Lou Dobbs' prestigious space.com site. Every one of these outreaches into traditional media builds a foundation for cracking through to the next level of attention.

How long did it take to actually get the attention of your targets?

Sometimes, I'll get a response to a query email immediately. I mean, SECONDS later. And sometimes two or three months will go by and then I may hear something. It all depends on timing.

Were the reporters you dealt with informed about the comics industry? If not, what did you do to bring them up to speed? Did your approach work?

Most of the folks I've dealt with have at least a passing interest in the comics industry. I think that's a pretty safe assumption to make, as the comics industry isn't exactly the highest profile in most people's consciousnesses. If a reporter is assigned a story he hasn't instigated, most are professional enough to do a little backgrounding before they respond to you or make an initial call.

Did the reporters let you talk about other comics works that you didn't create? If they did, did any of that information appear in the final product?

Sure. I try to give an overview of why I like comics in general, I enthuse about my favorite comics, and then I talk about the comics we publish. It helps to give a little context for the reporter and for the reader.

Did the reporters stick just to the work, or did they ask you about your life, your hobbies, your family, et. al.?

Sure. Most reporters want to give a context. I don't mind telling people I'm 37, and I'm married, and I own a house in San Francisco, one of the most competitive real estate markets in the country. I hope it helps to take the edge off the comic book fan stereotype of the 45 year old *Green Lantern* fan living in his parents' basement.

How do you feel about the entire publicity process?

This is kind of an interesting question. I am of two minds, in that I think publicity of any sort is, at best, sort of a necessary evil. On the other hand, I'm pretty good at it, so it's hard not to take satisfaction if not even a little pride in something you do well. If it helps sell our comics to people, I guess, at the end of the day, I'm all for it.

Any idea if the publicity helped or hurt your product?

Since we produce and market comics to compete with the premiere vendors in the comic book marketplace, I get a lot of good-natured "who does he think he is?" from comic book industry insiders, so maybe people who don't know what we're about may think all the attention is crass, or something. But traditional real-world media attention is nothing but good. If an article or news squib or even my astronautsintrouble.com email address showing up in *Entertainment Weekly* gets even one person into a comic store, I'm all for it. To a regular joe, the three dollars he's got to take out of his pocket to buy my book is the same three dollars he's got to spring for a *Batman*.

Is there such a thing as Too Much?

Not to me! I'm not going to rest until every man, woman, and child has got at least one copy of a comic we publish. And *Transmetropolitan*, too. Man, I love that comic. :)

When does a creator promoting the work cross the

line and become a creator unable to shut up about himself? Should this even be a concern?

Well, I am a little shameless, I have to admit, about promotion. But, as I said earlier, we have sunk a good amount of money into the publishing business, and we'd be doing ourselves a disservice if we didn't promote the work. And even moreso now that we are publishing other projects, like *Nobody, Channel Zero, Space Beaver,* and the like. We'd be doing a disservice to our other children if we didn't fire up the Marketing Machine.

And the Jimmy Carter Question - anything else you'd like to say?

Just that I find the comic book industry a little unique when it comes to its love-hate relationship with marketing and promotions. I think it has something to do with the American cowboy ideal of the strong, silent type letting his good deeds speak for themselves. Somehow, culturally, that morphed into the art world, where capital A art looked down its collective nose at commercialism, and a schism developed between those who create art for art's sake, and those who wouldn't mind eating something for dinner besides Raman noodles. I have an interesting perspective, because I've worked in advertising, marketing, publishing, and promotions for almost seventeen years, and I've seen a LOT of admen who are so good at what they do, there's no way you could classify it as anything BUT art. Once you create art, it needs an audience. Even if it's an audience of one, the artist who created it, art doesn't exist without the observer. I just unapologetically want as many observers of our art as possible, and marketing and promotion is an integral part of that.

And that, my friends, is a TRUE FACT.

eleven

Ever since I was a kid, I've been a Third Option kinda guy.

I guess it was just the way our parents raised us. Think outside the box. Stay on your toes. Show a little spine.

When my family went out to dinner, if I couldn't decide between the steak and the veal, I'd flirt with the waitress and order Chicken Cordon Bleu.

When I was in college, and the two Irish-Catholic lasses I was dating started to become more than I could handle, I started dating Pam Fishman, instead.

When I go out for a pint with the boys at Comix Experience, we don't look at a glass and think it's half full; nor do we think it's half-empty. We look at that glass and think it's time to call the barmaid over for another round.

The Third Option.

So.

Comics are dead dead dead. The best-selling comic on Diamond's charts now sells at a level that got *Omega The Unknown* cancelled less than twenty years ago.

Or, conversely, comics are vibrantly alive, what with this being an amazing time for envelope-pushing and diversity in comics. Alan Moore's ABC line. Warren Ellis' secret plans. Jim Mahfood's street cred.

Quality projects. Flat sales.

It's time to be courageous. To show a little spine.

It's time for the Third Option.

You may know that I write and publish a series of comics under the umbrella title *Astronauts in Trouble.* It's a good-looking package, with frankly kick-ass art by *The X-Files* and *X-Men: Hellfire Club* artist Charlie Adlard. Maybe you've seen the promotions I do for it online.

Know what I would hear almost unanimously when we would release a monthly chapter?

"I can't wait to read this; but I'm gonna wait for the trade."

Leaving aside the inherent silliness of that statement (what Ye Olde Editor Matt Fraction likens to folks saying, "Man, that *Space Cowboys* looks awesome; I can't wait until that comes out on video"), I have to admit it didn't take me long to stick up my metaphorical finger and see which way the proverbial wind was blowing.

Since what is laughingly referred to as "he comic book reading audience," having been weaned on a steady diet of MTV smash cuts, *Max Headroom*-esque blipverts, and the instant gratification the daily thumb exercise in front of Winston Smith's PlayStation provides... since this generation we call X is a product of its environment, I soon came to understand that what folks are looking for in their comics nowadays is not the serial nature of the unending soap opera of the funny books of years past, but a digestible piece of narrative with a discreet beginning, middle, and end.

And RIGHT NOW.

Now, everyone knows that I have control over my own

properties, and that *Astronauts in Trouble* is immune from the vagaries of economics that govern whether or not, say, your average DC miniseries will be reprinted in a trade paperback collection. Everyone knows that the monthly books function as loss leaders, proving to the marketplace that we can put out our quality entertainment on a monthly schedule, proving to retailers and fans alike that our books come out when we say they will.

But we've proved that already, so you might as well wait for the trade, ('cause you know your Wild Uncle Lar can't wait to package his issues into a nice big paperback with a new cover by somebody cool, and a compelling intro by a comic book bigshot, maybe a couple of pinups or a two pager drawn by a funky artist... you *might as well* wait for the trade, because the thing'll be a couple of dollars cheaper, it'll look better and be easier to find up there on your bookshelf, and there always seems to be at least one trade a week at the store on New Comics Day, so you can get your four-color fix then, anyway...

...so you may as well wait for the trade, and blow off those monthly issues. Save some time and money and energy.

Well, guess what?

I'm with you.

Why do monthly issues *at all?* Pay the artists extra for the covers, and the coloring? Pay the designers to format everything for as many issues of the monthly that comes out? That many PREVIEWS solicitations, that many PREVIEWS ads, that many press releases? For something most cats are just gonna ignore until the trade comes out anyhow?

Instead of doing 24 pages of art and story a month, why not do 72 pages of NEW stuff every three months? It's still the same rate of new material, but this way a reader's got the whole story; beginning, middle, and end... right there.

The monthly issues sit around for three months anyway, what with them being independent books. They either get snatched up right away by discriminating readers, or wait there lonely for three months, getting dog-eared and beat up until a rabid fan finds it after looking for it all over the Tri-State area. Why not guarantee a finished story every three months? It's a bold move, sure; but sometimes ya gotta show a little spine.

People are still coming in every Wednesday for their new books... with a little extra elbow grease on the slide rule to figure out the print management and scheduling, even DC could do nothing but 72-pagers for the rest of its corporate life. Imagine Superman coming out only four times a year... but DAMN if that wouldn't be an event. Those would be some KICK-ASS Superman stories. The Batman 72-pager the next week; the Wonder Woman 72-pager the week after that. Special projects and lesser lights in the pantheon sprinkled throughout.

The same VOLUME of entertainment. With more variety to the offerings.
Just think about it.

Us? Oh, we're doing it already. The comic book in its serialized pamphlet form is a dinosaur whose body doesn't know its brain is dead yet. Us clever mammals have already realized that original graphic novels are the model of comic book entertainment in the 21st century.

Most successful comic book stores are already operating on the bookstore model. Rory Root's Comic Relief in Berkeley, to just name one, is a bookstore that sells comics. Why not give Rory and the guys like him product to sell?

Comic books with a complete story. Perfect bound for long shelf life. UPC symbols and ISBN numbers, to make all the easier for regular bookstores to carry them, and a higher perceived value-for-the-dollar so even magazine racks and drug stores and barber shops and convenience stores can all make comics available again to the masses.

Our publishing house, AiT/Planet Lar, has kissed off the bloated corpse that is the monthly comic book pamphlet. We're publishing nothing but original graphic novels and collected trade paperback comic book entertainment from now on. We've said goodbye to staples.

It's time comic books showed a little spine.

And that, my friends, is a TRUE FACT.

•••••••••

I've got quite a soft spot for this one; this is the first time I put the public on notice, officially, that my publishing house was going to move over to a straight-to-trade paperback business plan. We'd done a lot of research on the viability of such a move, sure, and there'd been a few tentative steps from other houses towards this model, but no one had attempted so bold and so public a move at that time.

This is the one I point to when folks ask me when I realized that we had changed the rules and had taken advantage of the shift in comics fans' habits.

twelve

So, there we were, hanging about on the Larry Young Forum

http://forums.delphiforums.com/larryyoung/start

when Our Man Down Under, Mike Sims, suggested this week's column. He called it "What the Comic Book Industry Isn't: Ten Myths Debunked" and asked me to run my rant-like rampage over the sorts of things that most folks seem to take for granted.

So, I put it to the faithful and asked for the sorts of things upon which they wanted to see my take, he wrote, decidedly NOT ending the sentence with a preposition. Herewith, our first TRUE FACTS mailbag:

Erstwhile SAVANT editor Matt Fraction wants me to debunk these:

True or false—you need thousands and thousands of dollars to get a single issue out on the stands.

Well, it depends, on several factors: print run, whether you're paying artists and writers and letterers and colorists up-front money or making back-end deals... but I'm gonna say TRUE. It'll be at least a grand just to print a 24-page B&W comic with a print run that won't be negligible. It's important to be capitalized, when you start any business, and, make no mistake, comic book publishing is a BUSINESS. A good rule of thumb is to have six months living expenses AND six months operating expenses BEFORE you start. Otherwise, you may as well just buy lottery tickets, because if you don't your business has about the same chance of success.

True or false—Self-publishing isn't worth it, I should try to get signed by a major.

Also another "depends". Seems like Fraction has stock in adult diapers, or something. It really depends on what your goals and visions for your career are. If you just want to do a comic, do what I suggested way back in TRUE FACTS #1: Go ahead. No one's stopping you. If you are dying to write *Captain America,* Marvel's not going to hand him to you until you get a track record. So, hmmm… yeah, self-publishing is "worth it," as your chances of getting published go from nearly infinitesimal to one hundred percent.

True or false—Self-publishing is a financial and logistical nightmare, far too complicated for anyone save a selected, masochistic few to ever penetrate.

That's patently false. How the publishing world works is not a secret; you just have to pay attention. For painless instruction, check out the TRUE FACTS archives.

True or false—I am a beautiful and unique snowflake and everyone will want to read my book no matter what—the magic will just happen so I can sit back and hit the PlayStation until the checks come rolling in once the book is out there.

Urk.

True or false—I can fudge my deadlines and miss my ship-dates because the quality of my book is so great that the world will forgive me, or they will forgive me because I'm a self-publisher, doing it on my own, and everyone will understand how hard that is.

Sure. If you're a beautiful and unique snowflake.

Having had enough of Fraction's sarcasm, Ray Fawkes chimed in with: **True or False: it's possible to get significant awareness of your self-published proj-**

ect happening without spending thousands of dollars on advertising.

I'll go with "true" on this one, Ray. In fact, the 21st-century gossip-fest that is the Internet can help you get a level of attention to your project that was unheard of as little as ten years ago.

True or False: self-publishing is viewed with disrespect by editors in established companies.

Well, that hasn't been my experience. Most of the editors I've had occasion to speak to all are pretty amazed that anyone would even try publishing in the present climate in comics. And if you put out a high-quality book on a monthly schedule... there'll be no disrespect there, believe me.

Megan Thomas Bradner asks: **True/False? Editors have all the power.**

I'm gonna say "false" because of your use of the word "all." But there's nothing like a firm hand on the rudder to get your ship to go where it needs to sail. When I was writing *Astronauts in Trouble: Live from the Moon,* for example, I was starting to default into those corny James Bond-type jokes, which while briefly funny, tend to quash any building drama in a scene. Mimi Rosenheim, the editor on the project, handed down this edict: "Two stupid jokes an issue. That's it." And she was right. Made me handle some story tension in a better and more structured way, and improved the story immensely. She didn't step on my creativity, but she sailed the ship in the right direction. And that's what good editors do. Make sure your ship gets safely into port.

True/False? Color comics, how much do they really cost?

Roughly four times as much to produce as black-and-white comics, because you're not just printing black ink, but cyan, magenta, and yellow inks as well.

True/False? Previews - are they only game in town and do you have to play nice?

Well, if you don't get your project listed in PREVIEWS, you're not going to get a significant national distribution. And I play nice because that's how my parents raised me.

True/False? If you're not a spandex book, you'll never have sales like the big boys.

I think that *Sin City* puts the lie to that one.

True/False? No one wants to hear about another company that will be out of business in a year.

I think that one's true. Wouldn't you rather hear about good things happening in comics, than bad things like stores, and publishing houses, and distributors all closing up shop?

Patrick Keller, he of Internet ubiquity, writes: **"I would like you to debunk the myth that you don't sleep. Are you just really, really organized, or what?"**

Nope, I sleep. I am just really, really focused on writing and publishing good comics. I like designing good ads and writing compelling solicitation copy and making sure all the deadlines are met. I sleep, though. I sleep because I like waking up every morning and having my first thought be: "I get to write and publish more comics today." That's really just mind-blowingly cool.

And that, my friends, is a TRUE FACT.

thirteen

My good pal Bennett (he who had the tough-but-fair-minded, chiseled-jaw neo-hero of *Astronauts in Trouble: Live From The Moon* named after him) is having a bit of a mid-life crisis.

He's just turned 32, and with the poor powers of mathematics a public school edjimacation has left him with... well, he's figgered out that he's probably past the half-way point in his life. So he's taken up smoking cloves again, he's listening to KISS: LOVE GUN in an attempt to recapture those hazy days of youth, and he's given to asking otherwise unassuming gals if they wouldn't mind very much going out for a beer with him, because, really, aren't we all alone on this great big planet of ours and you might as well be drunk with a pleasant person of the opposite sex when all the shit comes down, which it's bound to any second, as I'm sure you'll agree, I get off at seven, I'll meet you there.

So, whilst giving the lad a good-natured ribbing about his abrupt about-face on the world in general and his once-surly ass in particular, ol' Bennett came up with what I thought was a particularly illuminating piece of bon, shall we say, mot. I was poking fun at him for being a veritable ray of sunshine now with his urbane cigs and smooth lines to the ladies, and I waxed nostalgic for the once-petulant babyhead that I'd grown to know and love.

And do you know what that tattooed, long-haired headbanger had the temerity to say to me? That which puts all sorts of things into perspective when you hear it?

"Ya can't have it both ways, Lar."

It dawned on me instantly that there weren't sadder words in the English language, because, while this truism is immediately obvious to the uninterested third-party, it is simultaneously human nature to want to have one's cake and eat it, too.

To wit.

Since you're reading this on SAVANT, chances are you've seen me around on the Internet, interjecting my opinions and basically rousing the rabble.

I'm still out there, lifting up the rotten log in the forest, poking my head under it to see what's going on, even though maybe I don't have time to respond to every little thing that tickles my fancy or raises my ire.

But I see what's going on. And it looks like everyone in comics wants it both ways.

God knows I love those gals over at www.sequential-tart.com, for example. The ones still there from the old days remember I was one of their most ardent supporters, right out of the gate.

But there's some wacky stuff going on over there on their message boards now. I was struck, the last time I coasted through, how a bunch of gals who WANT TO BE TAKEN SERIOUSLY... who want TO FOSTER A FEMALE PERSPECTIVE in an historically male-dominated industry... who have, pretty reliably, had the most intelligent, intuitive, and critical eye of any reviewers on the Internet I'd seen...

...have a humongous thread going over there about who they think is the sexiest man in comics.

Now, God bless 'em, they can knock themselves out, but...

...say it with me...

YOU CAN'T HAVE IT BOTH WAYS.

You can't want to be taken seriously and then write post after post about how some creator is dreamy. If, say, Brian Wood and I started a "sexiest chick in comics" thread on our respective message boards (that's
http://forums.delphiforums.com/larryyoung
and
http://forums.delphiforums.com/channelzero
respectively, for those interested) there would be a hue and there would be a cry, believe me. Something with the word "Neanderthal," I'd imagine.

But let's not single that sort of thing out. There are others. There is a growing movement on certain boards and on Usenet that "fans" are not happy with the interaction they have with the "pros."

Some say that a response from a "pro" is automatically loaded with an agenda, because said "pro"wants to sell you his comic.

Now, I'm an old cat. I'll be 37 in October, and I've been reading comics since before I could actually read. I still have the first comic I ever got: *Superboy* #145, when I was four years old.

So, I'm here to tell you that this is an amazing time for interaction between the folks who produce comics and the people who enjoy reading them. If there had been an Internet when I was fifteen or so, I'll bet you I'd have put out comics before I was twenty. I'd have been emailing Steranko and Archie Goodwin and Alex Toth and Will Eisner and Jim Shooter and George Tuska (actually, I really would have wanted to know whose idea it was to give *Iron Man* rocket skates) and

Stan friggin' Lee, trying to learn from them. And I would have soaked up every response like I was sitting at the feet of Socrates.

But there are those who say that ALL "pros" responses are suspect, because they just want to sell you comics. Now, God bless 'em, those folks can knock themselves out, but...

...say it with me...

YOU CAN'T HAVE IT BOTH WAYS.

Do people WANT responses, or do they want creators to return to their hovels in solitude and create the next comic for them to read, alone? Because it's only a matter of time before "pros" give up on providing content for the folks on the Internet to shoot at. For every thousand well-intentioned, articulate fans, there are four morons who spoil things for everyone else. A week or two ago, ol' Joe Casey wrote an impassioned but scattershot plea for belly-achers to put up or shut up, in his www.fandom.com column "Crash Comments"

But instead of writing ol' Joe and asking him to 'splain hisself, Casey got lambasted, called all sorts of names, and I'm pretty sure his lineage got called into question at least once. All over something that was pretty obvious if you read it twice.

Do you think Joe is going to want to respond to the next person who sends him an innocent email, now, after all of that?

And some people are decrying the supposed "monopoly" that Diamond has on the distribution arm of the comic book industry. "Facts" are purported to show that Diamond is responsible for all sorts of imbroglios, from holding a gun to Paul Levitz' head and making him shred comics, to the inability of right-thinking people to get a copy of *Battle Pope* #2, to the friggin' heartbreak of friggin' psoriasis. It just ain't so. Diamond's doing frankly yeoman work, and every single person who buys at least one comic a month should send an email to Diamond and THANK them for doing the job they're doing. Because they are doing it well.

Sure, things could always be better, there could be less intrigue and politics, and there might be less across-the-board agreement on Ben Raab... but all that's just human nature. We're all just a bunch of imperfect monkeys, and we can't have it both ways.

It's time for the comics community to look in the mirror, and pick a pitch and swing.

And that, my friends, is a TRUE FACT.

•••••••••

Interestingly, the folks who needed to get this message the most, at the time, had it completely lost on them, and the people who got their dander up the highest were the ones to whom this one applied the least.

I note that Joe Casey has pretty much withdrawn from a daily interaction with fans on the Internet, and, instead, prefers the one-step-removed outreach he gets by updating the interested on his movements on the

http://www.manofaction.tv

website.

fourteen

In addition to being married to the perfect girl and living in my own house in the best city in the world, one of the coolest things about being me is that our house is 30 yards from the best surfing in California north of Santa Cruz.

Many is the day I get up early and walk to Java Beach, a coffee house just down the way, and grab a hot steamin' cuppa joe and watch the morning surfers with all of the other hodads, thinking about my comic book empire.

Now, you know what a hodad is, don'tcha? That's a guy or gal who cheers on the surfers from the beach. Not like a wannabe, or a hanger-on, or a groupie, "hodad" isn't a pejorative at all. Surfers love their hodads.

And it occurred to me that all of the folks who write to me asking this or that are cheering us all on from the beach. So there shall be no more talk of "comic book fans" from me.

You are all hodads.

One such chap, who, oddly, asked to remain nameless, probably fearing the immense accolades and widespread public recognition he would have received for his excellent question, sent me an email slightly chiding me for my (he wrote) too-thorough job at shameless self-promotion. All in good fun, he asked me to use a column to define the difference between "promotion" and "self-promotion."

Well, that'd be a short column, I answered back, because there isn't one.

Write about that, then, he replied.

So.

Philosophically, I don't think there is any difference between "promotion" and "self-promotion." You have a product or good or service that you want folks to be aware of—one that will no doubt make their bleak and dreary lives better were they to purchase such from you.

As a practical matter, it doesn't matter if you produce or offer such for yourself or for a third party. But I understand the underlying inferences in asking about making such a distinction.

Many people find promoting themselves distasteful, but, again, as a practical matter, if you don't promote yourself, who will? I mean, really, in this media-saturated world, where hyped pseudo-events like the last episode of *Survivor* clears the streets for three hours because the hoi and the polloi don't want to be unplugged at the office water cooler, well, you can imagine how I personally have no problem pitching woo to the same folks.

But, there are ways to go about promoting your comic to the world that aren't distasteful, and don't seem, I dunno, boastful, I guess; or, worse, self-serving. First thing, you can keep track of your accomplishments. And I don't mean sending a press release to *Wizard* every time you mark something off your to-do list. I mean, every time you get a positive email, a good press clipping, or a stellar review of your work... SAVE IT. In no time, you'll have built yourself a big fat testimonial that other people have assembled for you. And, if you were to send out packages containing these testimonials, or quotes from them imbedded in press releases, well, that doesn't sound so boastful, now, does it, because it's ALEX ROSS saying you're an excellent artist, not you.

Another thing to keep in mind with this approach is to *target your audience.* Promotion gets under people's skin quicker if it's just a scattershot ego dump. There's no reason for me to tell the National Air and Space Museum that Warren Ellis and Garth Ennis like *Astronauts in Trouble;* I'd be better served telling them that Apollo lunar module pilot Rusty Schweickart's got a copy of the trade in his house. That's just good strategy.

You've got to be aware that promotion is an ongoing thing, as well. If you just pop into folks' lives whenever you've got a project to push, you're gonna look self-absorbed, or, worse, desperate. Just touch base with your peeps every once in a while, and it won't look jarring when you show up touting your latest genius.

One of the best things to do though, is to not be tempted to run in front of the snowball when it starts rolling without you. If your comic is as good as you say it is, eventually everyone else will notice, too. Some of the best self-promotion I've ever done has been knowing when to keep my mouth shut.

And that, my friends, is a TRUE FACT.

●●●●●●●●●●

Not a day goes by that I don't receive an email from someone calling me a "shameless self-promoter" or a "unapologetic self-publisher," even though my publishing and promotional efforts have long been relegated to works of others at our company: Warren Ellis, Brian Wood, Darick Robertson, Steven Grant, Jim Krueger, and the rest.

Proof, I guess, that the audience thinks I do possibly too good a job getting the word out...

fifteen

Enough of you cats have asked me recently either A. "What's a business plan?" or B. "What's YOUR business plan?" So, in a no-nonsense way to kill two birds with one stone, here's the complete answer to Question B (with all the pesky money-numbers removed) while simultaneously providing a template to Question A. Sorry if it's too nuts-and-bolts for some of you; I'll see you folks next week.

Otherwise, peek with me behind the curtain of the AiT/Planet Lar World Headquarters...

What is AiT/Planet Lar?

AiT/Planet Lar is a pop-culture company dedicated to bringing high-quality entertainment to the masses through the creation of original projects or producing works deserving of wider recognition. AiT/Planet Lar provides a full range of services from concept to completion including writing, art management, lettering, advertising and promotion, prepress production, ancillary merchandise, and print management.

Currently the company is focused on producing Original Graphic Novels to be distributed through mass-market bookstores, Amazon.com, and specialty bookshops around the world.

AiT/Planet Lar is:

Intelligent but not High-Brow
Boisterous but not Obnoxious
Intimate but not Cloying
Humorous but not Slapstick
Unconventional but not Obtuse

Vision Statement
Be a full-service entertainment conglomerate with mass-market appeal.

Strategic Priorities

Provide customers with superior, original entertainment that taps into the ever-changing zeitgeist of popular culture.

Create significant strategic partner relationships between businesses with similar visions that generate long-term value for both parties through leveraging each other's strengths.

Do what needs to be done. Break the rules to provide new and interesting products.

Continually innovate to predict and meet the needs of the market.

Shamelessly promote our products to bring them to a wider audience.

Focus on the few initiatives that provide the greatest value and implement them flawlessly.

Approach each project as the most important initiative and execute on it with the highest degree of professionalism.

Be leaders within the industry for knowledge, professionalism, and innovation.

Treat all creators, employees, and partners with respect and trust.

Continuously build the company brand and communicate its values.

Employ basic business practices to help guide all decisions.

Publish quality stories in the action/adventure and

science fiction genres.

Have fun.

Business Objectives for 2000-2001
Produce a product offered in nine of the next twelve months beginning in July, 2000.

Expand distribution of AiT/Planet Lar product line to mass retail outlets including Amazon.com, Virgin Megastores and one of the top 10 booksellers in the U.S.

Initiate a project to bring *Astronauts in Trouble* to rich media format by end of 2001

Expand ancillary product market into toy creation for the *Astronauts in Trouble* titles.

Increase revenue over 1998-1999 through publishing finished works, increasing distribution channels, selling high-margin products, and licensing the rights to AiT/Planet Lar-owned properties.

Take on no projects for previously published or finished works that do not promise to make a profit within the first three months of publication.

Publish Astronauts in Trouble titles in at least one other language by end of 2001.

Principals
Larry Young has been called the "Johnny Appleseed of Comics," has a B.A. in English from Clark University, and has worked in print since 1981. Young has the unique distinction of having daily involvement in all aspects of the comic book industry including creative, production, publishing, distribution and retailing. He is the Chief Visionary, Creative

Engine, and Marketing Guru for AiT/Planet Lar.

Mimi Rosenheim has a Mass Communication degree from Boston University and an MBA from University of San Francisco. She has worked with all forms of print and digital media in the last ten years, provides editorial guidance for original works and oversees the Financial, Operational and Business Development activities for AiT/Planet Lar.

sixteen

We have been warned.

I'm sure it's not escaped anyone's notice (surely not anyone who keeps track of the comic book industry's machinations, at least) that the sky, well, she's falling.

There've been stern lectures and harsh words and excuses ad nauseum, as well as pleadings and warnings and calls-'em-as-we-see-'ems.

Sorry.

Just channelling my inner model of a modern major general.

The point is, the numbers, they've been crunched. Trends have been identified. The right people have been spoken to. Everyone agrees.

Comics are dead. And you know, comics as we know them? As we've been accustomed to them?

They probably are.

But, y'know... what fun is that?

The fact is, nobody knows anything. It's like my Dad says as he cuts up his pepperoni and cheese and gets his chips and salsa together, when he's getting ready to watch a football game and I ask him who he thinks is going to win.

"Nobody knows," he always says, "that's why they play the games."

I remember I went to go see Dave Sim at some mall store in Springfield, Massachusetts, around the time the Wolverroach issues of *Cerebus* were out. It was a

Sunday, he had a pretty big hangover. I went with the girl I was dating then and my roommate Rob. The girl couldn't remember what kind of animal Cerebus was, and Rob gave me his stack of *Cerebus* #1-13 to read in the first place. Girl hasn't been heard from since 1986 and Rob was in my wedding. Coincidence? I think not.

Anyway.

Rob and I were chatting with Dave and he was incredibly cool considering he had been so drunk the night before. By that time the 300-issue brag was on the table, and my ol' pal Rob told Dave he didn't think he was going to be able to do it, and the comics folks we knew pretty much didn't think it was going to happen, either.

There was an audible gasp from the folks in line.

Dave looks up, bleary-eyed. Then a slow smile starts to creep in. More of a grin, really. A self-satisfied smirk. The twinkle of some profound inner truth. The crowd waits...

"Huh," says Dave.

And y'know, that just cracked me up.

When you have your eye on the ball, when you're (and you know I hate to say it) being the bunny, it kinda doesn't matter what anyone else thinks. And it looks like Dave is going to finish up in March of 2004, doing what he's been doing since December of 1977. So that doesn't mean that every jackass who says he's going to put out his comic actually will. It doesn't mean that a corporate mis-step will get The Unluckiest Man in Comics fired. It doesn't mean that monthly pamphlets are a dinosaur who doesn't know it's brain is dead yet. It doesn't mean that comics produced independently from Marvel or DC will save the artform...

It just means you never know.

I'm a pretty big San Francisco Forty-Niners fan. Went to the last pre-season game they played. Buffalo, I think. I don't remember, because the Niners sucked and the missus and I spent the game talking to this old crust who had the seat next to me, and he spent the game telling us obscure Niners facts. Some were great, and others were dry and not very interesting. I spent those anecdotes looking around at the 40,000 people dressed up as their favorite players and pondered whether or not if there were 40,000 people in one place dressed as Klingons and Vulcans and waving United Federation of Planets flags in such a frenzy the authorities wouldn't just bomb the place to make sure they didn't sully the gene pool.

Anyway, this guy starts going on about how the Niners sucked worse than this back when Coach Seifert was only the defensive assistant, and he would drill the kids even after practice, and then make them watch films and fire questions and just try to impart his enthusiasm by osmosis, if he had to. Because no one cared about these rookies and the expectations were so low for them the guys reading the sports pages and calling the radio shows figured they'd all be gone or hurt by the end of the second year so they were all gonna go fishing until then because the Niners were just going to suck.

Except the three rookies and the nobody in the defensive backfield forgot that they were supposed to be scared and inexperienced and sucky, and Ronnie Lott (who's in the Hall of Fame now), and Eric Wright, who was probably the finest coverage back when he was on his game, and some guy named Williamson (whose first name I forget, and I'm gonna get slammed by a football fan, I know) and Dwight Hicks became the hellhounds of the League that year and helped some kid named Montana win his first Lombardi.

Now, I'm trying to remember how many sports page guys and radio call-in show listeners and Vegas odds-makers and company football pool players all predicted that one, but it wasn't a whole lot if you know what I mean and I think you do.

It just means you never know. That's why we do it.

So, I'm gonna go finish the lettering on the last bit of art I just got from Charlie Adlard for the trade paperback *Astronauts in Trouble:One Shot, One Beer*, which is coming out from us at the end of October.

Then I'm gonna read the bluelines of the *Channel Zero* trade paperback again (out in stores September 13th), just because I can.

Because if the sky is falling for Marvel and DC and Dark Horse and Image and whoever, you guys are gonna need comics to read. We might just be the last men standing. 'Cause you never know.

And that my friends, is a TRUE FACT.

•••••••••

I tried to strike an inspirational and simultaneously informational tone with these columns, but I wrote this one for me. As I recall, we were heading into a particularly volatile phase when it was first written, and this one was a re-statement of purpose, directly from me to Fate. Fate then blinked and shuddered under my onslaught of comics' righteous anger.

seventeen

So, we were hanging out at Comix Experience last Friday, and Ed and Jeff and Rob and I were having our usual "Breakfast of Champions" - good Scotch in bathroom cups and Bass Ale out of the bottle - when ol' Darick comes in to say goodbye as he's heading back to New Yahk City.

So we pour him a libation and toast each other and take long pulls off the Bass to chase the Scotch, and I have just enough time to reflect on how beer is like liquid comics when the phone rings.

"Caaaaahmixexperience," I say.

"Yeah, I got a bunch of comics I want to sell. I've got.."

""Easy, cha-cha," I interrupt, having had this conversation hundreds of times with hundreds of people. "You know the drill, right? How we buy comics?"

"Er, no," says the guy on the other end of the phone. "But I've got a poly-bagged Death of Superman..."

"So do two-and-a-half million other people. This is what we do. You bring in your comics. We don't even look at them. We have a freight scale here and we load 'em up. We put 'em on the scale and give you fifty cents a pound."

One of two things happen, here, at this point in the conversation, and both are entertaining. One reaction, and may I say, depending on my mood, the preferred reaction, is, "Wow. Great. Awesome. I was just gonna throw out this trash; I mean this whole long box was just taking up space and I don't feel like lugging it over to my new apartment."

"Well, a long box, depending on what kind of paper is

in it, will get you about $15-$20," I'll say.

"And you take it all?"

"Yep, that's the brilliance of it. You don't have to lug it around to five or six stores where they'll cherry pick the stuff they really want, leaving you with ten bucks and 200 comics left over. We'll take all 350 for a flat rate and you can go live your life with a just and knowing smile knowing that someone, somewhere, will give your complete run of Micronauts a good and happy home."

Half the time, people will bring in boxes of shoes or old games or something, too, thinking we're some kind of pawn shop or salvage house. But because there's nothing but comics and trade paperbacks in Comix Experience, the atmosphere of the store lends us its gravitas when we nod at the stack of funny books and say, "Just the comics. We only sell comics here."

But the other response is even more entertaining, if it's not too busy in the shop when we get the call.

The phone'll ring, and I'll say, "Caaaaahmix experi- ence."

"Yeah, I got a bunch of comic books I want to sell. I've got..."

"Easy, cha-cha," I interrupt, having had this conver- sation hundreds of times with hundreds more people in the time between the last call. "You know the drill, right? How we buy comics?"

"OK, sure, I know you won't want everything, but I've got all five covers of the Jim Lee X-Men #1..."

"Yep; but so do two-and-a-half million other people," I'll say. "I don't want to waste your time, man. We buy comics by the pound. No matter what you have, we throw 'em on our scale and give you fifty cents a pound. Don't even look at 'em."

When there is dead silence on the phone, I look around to see if there are a lot of customers in the store. If there are, and it'll get busy, this is a short conversation, because of its binary finality. People are either going to sell their comics for fifty cents a pound or they won't. If I don't have time to go into it, I won't. You're either on the bus or you're not.

But if it's raining out, or it's a slow morning, I like to have a little fun on the phone with these people. Because they think I haven't had this same conversation hundreds of times with hundreds of people before *they* called.

"What?" they'll begin, usually thinking I'm either kidding or they've misheard or something.

"When you come in with your stack of comics, we have a little freight scale sitting there waiting. I take your comics and put them on the scale. I offer you 50 cents for every pound of comics."

"But... but... these are GOOD ones. They're in plastic bags and everything."

"Oh," I will say, nonchalantly, "that's different." This gets 'em going until: "I have to subtract 10% for that, because the bags add weight. We can't use old bags. Just comics." More silence. Until the explosion.

"AREYOUKIDDINGME?" it usually begins. "IBOUGHT THESEFORTHREEBUCKSAPIECE!DOYOUKNOW WHATTHESEARE WORTH?"

And I love that one, because there IS an answer to that. "Yep," I'll say. "Fifty cents a pound."

And this is the bit that separates the men from the boys. Because if you want to talk about VALUE, comics are priceless. When I ask somebody what time it is, and they say, "3:37," I don't think it's almost four o'clock.

I think that's the first Walt Simonson issue of *Thor* and I'll remember the Marvel house ad I saw a couple of months before that that Walt drew, showing Thor standing on a pile of vanquished Frost Giants with his tunic ripped and his leggings unwrapped, and how I finally realized that those actually WERE leggings instead of some odd Kirby patterns on his boots.

Or how when I buy a pack of gum and some Slim Jims and the clerk says, "That'll be $2.52," I always think that's the *Amazing* with the first appearance of the black costume and how odd it was we had to wait seven months to finally see how Spidey got it in *Secret Wars* #8. I can tell you what I was doing when I got Dark Knight Returns #1. I can tell you which page I was looking at when I finally realized my boyhood dream to be Stan Lee had finally come true.

And there are at least 500,000 other cats in the U.S. just like me. So if you want to talk about the VALUE of comics, I gotta say that the artform, the physical objects, the joy and entertainment they provide... well, it's all priceless.

But what are they actually *worth?*

It's fifty cents a pound.

And that, my friends, is a TRUE FACT.

eighteen

Your assignment for this week is to purchase and read these two books:

Rules for Revolutionaries, by Guy Kawasaki.

Published by Harper Business, its ISBN is 0-88730-995-X

and

Digital Pre-Press for Comic Books, by Kevin Tinsley.

Published by Stickman Graphics, its ISBN is 0-9675423-0-8

If I had had these two books in 1988, I would be running Marvel editorial today instead of Joe Quesada.

Seriously.

If you want to make a mark on comics, it's all here in these two books for the folks who can hear the message.

I'll see you next week to tell you why.

And that, my friends, is a TRUE FACT.

nineteen

Two weeks ago, I recommended a couple of books for you to check out, if you seriously want to make your own comics.

The first, *Rules for Revolutionaries,* by Guy Kawasaki, offers up innovations that you can use in any industry, but which I found to be quite useful if applied to comics.

Split into Brancusi's three categories, the book offers these "rules," which are not so much rules as Zen-like koans upon which to ruminate as you enact your plan for world domination.

Create like a God. Command like a King. Work like a slave.

These three sentences resonate for me.

Further, any book which quotes this Apple advertising copy as its foreword is OK with me: "Here's to the crazy ones, the misfits, the rebels, the troublemakers, the round pegs in square holes, the ones who see things differently. They're not fond of rules, and they have no respect for the status quo. You can quote them, disagree with them, glorify or vilify them. About the only thing you can't do is ignore them, because they change things. They push the human race forward, and while some may see them as the crazy ones, we see genius, because the people who are crazy enough to think they can change the world are the ones who'll do it."

When last week's TF guest columnist suggested I read *Rules for Revolutionaries,* the title put me off right away. "Right," I thought, "some dumbass MBA is going to tell me the 'rules' for me to follow to be revolutionary. Talk about *unclear on the concept.*"

Then I read the foreword, and I was hooked.

You really should read it and glean the gems out for yourself, but here's a few things I really liked:

In describing the revolutionary thought process, Kawasaki urges you to forget your idols and purge yourself of the old habits of your business. He tells you to change your framing so as your business defines the marketplace instead of being defined by it.

Another good one is to prod others to see your vision. A few weeks back, on Warren Ellis' superior comic book industry resource (from which even Savant herself hath sprung), www.delphiforums.com/ellis, I started a discussion thread called "COMICS: What's pissing you off?" as a direct result of reading this bit of Kawasaki's book.

There were over 300 answers to that question in two days, proving to me that the comic book industry is on the cusp of a Big Change.

And if you want to be an Agent of Change, you need to read this book and apply its lessons to the vision you have of your industry.

OK, so let's say you've been inspired by Kawasaki, you've read through his book, you've got a clear vision of where you see yourself, and you are ready to drive the comic book train down a new set of tracks.

The next book you should absolutely get is Digital Pre-Press for Comic Books, by Kevin Tinsley.

The reason I first offered my services to Savant is because I was getting a frankly stunning number of emails asking me what THE SECRET to doing comics was. No one wanted to hear, "Well, hard work." Or, the more complete, "I've been involved in mainstream marketing, advertising, promotions, and print publishing for almost eighteen years. I'm just applying my aggregate knowledge of these fields and bringing 'em to bear in comic books."

No one wants to hear that, because human nature is not wired that way, and is probably in our race memory from when the first caveman went out and said, "Hey, Korg, I'm sick of eating berries. I'm gonna go out and get me a mastodon tenderloin."

Since then, human nature has been all about the shortcut. If you want to know all about comic book-specific DTP, it's in Tinsley's book.

From definitions of terminology, to standard formats of digital files, to scanning resolutions, dot gain, digital lettering, Quark bleed dimensions, color seps, vectors, page compositions, cover layout, PhotoShop comps, and artists' alterations, EVERY SINGLE THING YOU NEED TO KNOW ABOUT COMIC BOOK PRODUCTION is in this single book, written by a former Marvel bullpenner.

You should buy this book not just for the no-nonsense delivery of absolutely essential facts, not just for the time it'll save you getting up to speed, but because you should get your DTP advice from Tinsley who is fluent with comic book digital pre-press like he's speaking his mother tongue, instead of from me, ancient bastard that I am.

Your local shop could do worse than have a couple of these on its how-to rack. Let 'em know they'll be doing the next Dave Sim a big favor.

And that, my friends, is a TRUE FACT.

twenty

Now that we've elected a new President, and probably not coincidentally, have reformatted the look-and-feel of SAVANT a little bit, it's time to get back into the swing of things.

Over the hiatus, I got to thinking quite a lot about customer service in general, and the said dropping of the ball on Marvel's part in particular. I quickly dismissed this topic as the source of my first column back, until I read a bit about the ancient Greeks in Harvey Mackay's excellent business column "Swimming with Sharks."

It seems as though in the ancient city of Athens, when young, well, Athenians reached the voting age, they were compelled by obligation to a sense of civic duty to stand in the public square, in front of all good gentlemen and true, and take this oath:

"We will strive unceasingly to quicken the public sense of duty - so that we will make this city greater, better, and more beautiful than it was when we took this oath."

Well, I have to say I had to wipe away a manly tear when I read this, because if you replace "this city" with "the comic book industry," that's pretty much how I feel about what I do. So when I see someone dropping the ball on something that's an easy fix, well...

...let's just say I think all good gentlemen and true have a civic duty to shine God's Flashlight into the corners, and make the comic book industry a holy place again.

So let's roll up the sleeves, shall we?

Marvel has lost touch with who their customers are.

Now whether you believe Marvel's customers are the retailers who buy their books initially or the fans who buy them as end-users, the point remains.

So instead of outlining the full litany of INCREDIBLY SILLY BUSINESS DECISIONS Marvel has made in just the last six weeks (including Jemas stating that they wouldn't reprint Ultimate Spider-Man #1 to fulfill immediate demand so as to make it a twenty-dollar book on the after-market; posting the book on the marvel.com site so as to drive eyeballs to their advertising and thereby cut out retailers who could have ridden the wave of interest Marvel was accruing in the mainstream press; the X-MAN/AOL miscue; and the very public airing out of the *FF: Big Town* debacle resulting in Marvel posting PRESS RELEASES on their own site, thereby turning their web presence into a newsroom); no, instead of listing their transgressions, I'm gonna help Marvel out here with a little treatise on customer focus and service.

Because I care.

It is in the best interests of every creator, publisher, distributor, and retailer that Marvel remain a going concern. It is in the best interests of us all that the comic book industry is run by folks on the top of their games.

Because we are in a time of flux, here.

So I'll even keep this general so anybody reading this can apply this to any business. In fact, you could apply this to your personal life, even, because good customer focus is very much like building a relationship.

When a company is customer-focused, it's got every individual in the company, regardless of function, from the folks in the mail room to the guy in the Big Chair, deeply understanding who it is who uses their products or services, why they are using their products or services, and will never make a decision without understanding the full impact on the end-user of their products or services.

Nothing here yet to argue with, eh? Who wouldn't agree that being customer-focused is important?

But I don't think Marvel has a clear view of who their customers are.

The products they offer are all over the map. It looks to me (a guy who writes comics, publishes comics, distributes comics, and sells comics; a guy who drives the whole train from concept to completion) that they're just throwing stuff against the wall and seeing what sticks.

They publish print comics. But they also post them online, where your consumer of print works and online content are usually two different sets of folks. Now, of course, I'm not privy to Marvel's business practices, but you can bet the farm they're selling content to vertical aggregator sites, too.

That's three different definitions of "customer" right there.

Now, when I was a kid, Stan and Jack and Sol and Flo were the folks giving my comics to me. Ol' Stan served up a world of like-minded cats in a haze of camaraderie, weaving their tales direct from New York City to my back yard treehouse.

Well, guess what?

Those Rockwellian salad days have gone the route of

the 9600 baud modem, and even the most Luddite of comics fans knew about the impending reshuffling of the Counter-X books BEFORE THE CREATORS ON THE VERY BOOKS THEMSELVES.

Technology has changed the comic book landscape, and Marvel is still acting like it's 1965.

They need to have a unified voice on the comic book news sites and other information channels on the Internet. The solution to almost any difficulty can be boiled down to "better communication."

If Marvel doesn't already have a cross-functional Customer Task Force within their company, they should start one.

Composed of upper management and editorial heads, they should establish and articulate the importance of customers within the company, and speak with one voice to the assembled halls of Marveldom.

Because, you know, to this observer, it looks like they're all worried more about who's stronger... The Hulk? Or Thor?

Where have you gone, Stanley Leiber? The Merry Marvel Marching Society turns its lonely eyes to you. Woo, woo, woo.

The day is coming when those companies not speaking with one voice are going to be drowned out by those with a laser-like sense of purpose.

And that, my friends, is a TRUE FACT.

••••••••••

I love Marvel Comics. I'm direct, because I care.

twenty-one

One of the many things I've noticed as a comic book publisher...

Wait; strike that.

One of things that stands out in comics like a pretty girl at a bus stop is that the marketing of funny books is intertwined with the very identity of the publishing company. Successful marketing is being done by those who realize that marketing is no longer an isolated function of a company, but an integrated part of the whole.

The best marketing in any industry is being done by those who have the clearest vision for their company. Look at Bill Gates. The CEO of Microsoft is practically their Chief Marketer as well. A guy like me who reads the papers can't spot a difference between Microsoft's corporate strategy and their marketing strategy. It goes hand in hand.

But for the life of me, I can't figure out where Marvel's going. And I'm afraid their lack of direction is going to kill the comics industry.

They weren't able to co-opt the attention they got from the success of THE X-MEN movie; they let Stan Lee out of his exclusivity deal, and the first thing ol' Stan did was sign up with DC...

They got mainstream media attention for ULTIMATE SPIDER-MAN # 1... and *deliberately* kept it out of print; they poly-bagged an old version of AOL software to an issue of X-MAN... and then *the very next week* they let their AOL-only content site lapse...

...I mean, I could go on.

Seems to me Marvel doesn't know who it is, anymore.

I have some insight into this, albeit on a smaller scale, of course. Our publishing house, AiT/Planet Lar, is constantly working to refine and underline its identity in the comic book marketplace. We offer high quality trade paperbacks containing self-contained stories featuring science fiction and action-adventure with an interesting twist.

If a reader is browsing the shelves in his local comics store, and sees a collection of illustrated Grateful Dead lyrics, for example, that reader might not be able to tell you who the publisher was without looking at the spine, but he could tell you that it *wasn't* an AiT/Planet Lar book, because that sort of thing is off-brand for us. We have a clear vision for our company, and we stick to it.

But I'd be willing to bet that if you asked twenty different Marvel employees what the Marvel brand was, you'd get twenty different answers. And even then, it seems as though Marvel believes that if only their characters were more well-known, they would be more successful. But as this summer's big-budget X-MEN movie proved, the characters can be very well-known and not make the publishing company any money. The characters can be well-known and not be able to sell funny books.

As a comic book entrepreneur and rakish impressario, I can tell you authoritatively that success in the comic book marketplace is based on *disloyal* customers. Why would one start a new publishing company if you didn't believe you could take customers away from where they are now? What's the only way a publisher is going to get marketshare away from a competing publisher?

Put out *better comics.*

Keeping readers is a temporary phenomenon. That doesn't mean that companies can't keep their readers; DC has done a heck of a job turning *Sandman* readers into *Preacher* readers into *Transmet* readers into *Outlaw Nation* readers. But that's a sort of eat-your-young spiral, and the thing separating DC from Marvel is its impressive backlist.

But, really, since comics are becoming more and more at parity (I mean, really; what's the difference between Supreme, Mr. Majestyk, and Superman?), even putting out better comics might not be enough. Companies have to think about multiple forms of access, and this is one area where Marvel really excels.

The X-MEN movie of this summer; the WB EVOLUTION cartoon; the ubiquitous Toy Biz action figures all have decent market penetration...

...but they don't provide straight-line access back to the comics.

Why wasn't there an X-Men giveaway comic in every movie house that screened the flick, as an entry point for new readers? Why was the TV GUIDE story so impenetrable? Why isn't www.the-master-list.com up on the screen at the end of every cartoon? Why isn't the back of every Spider-Man blister pack not a billboard for more action figures, but a few panels of Spidey in action and a coupon for the latest issue?

It's all about access.

How the hell has AiT/Planet Lar sold eight times as many CHANNEL ZEROs as the Image version?

It's all about *access*.

We let people know we had them, and we made it easy for them to get them. How did we create readers for a book that had already been released into the comic book marketplace? We had a presence, just like a Wal-Mart, an ATM, a Coke machine; we had a place in your computer.

We told folks online that they could order them from their retailer, and made sure Diamond was fully stocked. Can't get to your retailer? Well, they're on www.amazon.com, too.

We got mainstream press in *Wired* for it, and when folks came looking for the book, we put 'em in their hands.

Why can't Marvel do this, instead of keeping stuff unavailable on purpose? It just seems odd that AiT/Planet Lar has a better access infrastructure than the home of *Spider-Man* and the *Hulk*.

Marvel has to figure out who they are, recognize the value of what they offer their customers, streamline their access channels, and funnel customers back into reading comics again, or you're gonna be reading "LARRY YOUNG PRESENTS CAPTAIN AMERICA" within ten years.

And that, my friends, is a TRUE FACT.

●●●●●●●●●●

As our company became more successful, I began to better understand the challenges Marvel faces. It's easy for outside obsevers to comment on the public actions of a corporate entity; it's a bit harder for those observers to get a good grasp on what's really going on. I remain convinced a well-run Marvel Comics is necessary for a healthy comics industry.

twenty-one

Good night, sweetheart; it's time to go.

Yep, that's right; this is the last TRUE FACTS.

But that's not a bad thing. It's good. It just means you guys don't need me anymore.

When I first started doing these for Fraction and Potter and Austin, I only thought I'd do four of 'em. One on pre-press, one on printing, one on distribution, and one on retailing. But it became clear to me that whenever I wrote one, it would suggest two or three other columns, and Fraction suggested we do it ongoing and I thought that wasn't such a bad idea, because I really liked what the Savants were doing, and I figured it wouldn't hurt to give 'em a little content. 'Course, I liked that I could write about publishing and have a place to point folks who wanted to know the secret to success in comics.

Oh, I'll be around. I'm sure something'll piss me off and I'll send a column to Fraction, and he'll laugh so hard that *two* drops of pee'll come out as he codes it up for the Savant audience to read.

I'm sure you'll see something by me in the letters section most weeks, because I'm that kinda guy... and like as not I'll be posting my special brand of wackiness on the Savant message boards at:

www.delphi.com/savantmag/messages

There just won't be a *weekly* TRUE FACTS. But I'll be around. Your Wild Uncle Lar has his eye on you all.

My job here is through.

And that, my friends, is a TRUE FACT.